HOW TO BE A CHIEF RETIREMENT OFFICER (CRO)

Preparing Your Business for the Retirement Boom Ahead

by Thomas Rowley

President and Publisher: Mitch Anthony
Contributing Editor: Bobbye Middendorf
Senior Managing Editor: Debbie Anthony
Project Editor: Suzanne Norby, MD
Interior Design: Greg Wimmer
Illustration: Greg Wimmer
Cover Design: Greg Wimmer

Published by Advisor Insights Press

Printed in the United States of America

ISBN: 0-9727523-2-3

DEDICATION

Thank you to my parents Dr. Eugene and Jane Rowley, and my extended family for faith in me. To my wife Trish, and my children Colin, Andrew, and Ellie for patience and love, you are my inspiration.

CONTENTS

PREFACE

Over the past 20 years, I have been employed in the retirement business of the financial services industry—an arena that has experienced dramatic changes over that period. From the basic premise of who is in charge of funding retirement (individuals are, now!), to methods of funding (anyone still remember the HR-10, KEOGH, and SAR-SEP?), and to the constantly changing rules and regulations (TRA86 to EGTRRA), we're traveling at high speed down a twisting river filled with the rocks and rapids of change.

I have always been in the role of answering the questions of my fellow financial professionals. Early on, I worked at a "Retirement Answer Desk." There, the questions were specific technical and operational questions. "What are the rules regarding...?" from IRAs to qualified plans. I graduated to a marketing role, and the questions became strategic: "I've got a client, and he's trying to accomplish..." I moved on to selling. The questions from financial professionals included prospecting, selling, and servicing clients. Financial advisors are a sophisticated audience. They understand the big picture.

However, when I met "real people" like your clients, they were asking basic questions. I started doing 401(k) enrollments in the mid-1980s when people had never heard of a 401(k). I have done hundreds of enrollments, and the questions scared me. Here was a generation of people who are responsible for their own retirements. Most are not prepared and, moreover, are unaware that they are not prepared. It is not that they're not smart enough, or that the information is too complex. Most of your clients and prospects are suffering from the four Cs of modern life:

- *Constant change:* new rules, new ways, nonstop
- *Communication overload:* too much, too often; linked but not connected
- *Competition for attention:* more demands with increasing complexity
- *Compression of time:* trying to do more things in the same amount of time

It's as if people are trying to put together a puzzle. They have all the pieces but not the box with the picture on it. They stare at individual pieces trying to connect them, without knowing the big picture. Financial professionals hold the box with the picture on it. Therefore, this is a puzzle that can be solved, but most people do not make use of the financial professional who has the big picture at hand.

Enrolling people into their 401(k) plans became my mission. I figured that if they did not save for their retirement, the government would eventually tax me to pay for them. My main pitch was, "If you save a little bit of money over a long period of time, you will have more money saved than if you didn't."

To be truly effective, an enroller—like a financial professional—must be an educator, combining content knowledge with empathy, honesty, and humor. The breed apart also brings the power of a passionate belief in the work of building client wealth and helping to create someone's retirement dream.

When it comes to planning retirement, a well-qualified financial professional can be invaluable. The benefits of working with someone like you will reach beyond just choosing investments. A financial professional can help map out a long-range investment strategy using an asset allocation model—taking into account risk tolerance, time horizon, and tax consequences. Of all the choices your clients can make about their money, the choice to use a professional financial advisor may be the best decision.

Let me define what I mean by "financial professional." For my purposes, financial professionals possess a broad knowledge of the situations most individuals are likely to encounter in saving for retirement. They are able to translate this knowledge into a realistic plan. Whether they call themselves financial advisors, financial planners, agents, brokers, bankers, insurance agents, accountants, lawyers, or investment representatives, they bring skill, knowledge, expertise, and customer care to serve the needs of their clients.

Financial professionals should be good listeners who can identify clients' needs and desires in developing a plan. They must be able to apply the right solutions without hesitating to engage other professionals to fill in where their expertise ends. One thing I learned from the Retirement Answer Desk is that the best answer may be, "I don't know, but I know where to find out. Let me get back to you or put you in touch with those people."

Empathy requires you to read the emotional states, attitudes, and perceptions of your audience. Empathy is the ability to see others from their personal frame of reference and to communicate this understanding to the person involved. In order for financial professionals to establish a supportive relationship with their clients, they must be open and honest.

People are often reluctant to discuss money. If financial professionals are perceived as genuine, with a strong desire to listen, clients will open up and discuss their dreams, goals, and issues. Humor can also play an important part in the learning process. Humor can reduce tension. Shared laughter is a powerful way to reinforce learning, set people at ease, and increase rapport. So, expect some from me along the way.

In addition, a successful financial professional demonstrates a caring attitude. Caring consists of understanding a person's experiences while establishing a learning relationship with them. Ultimately, it is sharing yourself with another person in a way that makes a difference in both your lives.

As the 1990s drew to a close, another shift was taking place. The constantly varying workplace and retirement landscape became like the outer banks after a hurricane—all but unrecognizable. Since I starting writing this book at the end of 2002, the story I call "The Winds of Change" has blown in like the series of hurricanes that have hit the East Coast. The impending pension crisis I describe has accelerated quickly. From Big Steel, the crisis has moved to the airlines. The recent press regarding some airlines not wanting to continue to fund their pension plans while in bankruptcy is the next chapter of the story. If the Pension Benefit Guaranty Corporation (PBGC) takes over the United Airlines plan obligations, watch for the domino effect throughout the airline industry.

If the government guarantees an industry's liability, that industry will figure out how to shift the liability to the government. If the PBGC continues to take on the pension obligations of increasing numbers of failing companies, it will be unable to remain solvent. Of course, the government cannot let all these pensions go up in smoke. Remember the S&L bailout? That cost the American taxpayer somewhere between $150-200 billion. The PBGC is potentially next in line for a massive taxpayer-paid bailout. The time is now to protect your clients from *The Winds of Change* that I discuss in detail in the first section.

Observing all these changes bearing down on us like a hurricane, and at the same time frequently speaking, presenting, or training financial advisors at industry conferences, I was well-positioned to initiate the call for financial professionals to step in and become their clients' Chief Retirement Officer (CRO).

What is a CRO?

You're familiar with CEO, CFO, COO, and CIO, titles that recognize business executives at the highest level—the big leagues of executive leadership, finance, operations, and information. As retirement planning takes on increasing importance, your new title, CRO, reflects your role as the senior-level person on your clients' retirement advisory team. By summarizing the situation, clarifying options, and guiding them through the decision-making process, you will occupy a key advisory role, supporting clients as they accept increasing responsibility for funding an expanding life span and redefining retirement and old age.

The Chief Executive Officer (CEO) usually sets the direction and oversees the operations of an organization. This individual is responsible for carrying out the strategic plans and policies established by the board of directors. The Chief Financial Officer (CFO) is usually responsible for financial control systems and recordkeeping for a company.

Most of your clients and many of your prospects need a CRO. This acknowledges that your clients' relationship with you is a long-term partnership that will help them stay on track in meeting retirement goals. As CRO, you can help by understanding your clients' complete portfolios. This means analyzing suitable investments, keeping track of necessary paperwork, keeping up-to-date with rule changes, and continuously monitoring current status while anticipating changing needs. The CRO also brings to the table all the listening skills, empathy, honesty, humor, and caring attitudes that are the marks of top financial professionals.

I made up the term "Chief Retirement Officer" (CRO). Feel free to use it. I didn't trademark it. I would prefer that our industry fill with Chief Retirement Officers who are enthusiastically and passionately helping their clients plan and save for their retirements. Without this passion, you cannot succeed. While knowledge and experience can go a long way, they will never account for truly over-the-top success.

What really moves people is your belief in your work and the passion you bring to building relationships and creating winning retirements for your clients. I believe that a Chief Retirement Officer can do more good for more people and can make that good last far longer than almost any other professional. They need you!

Tom Rowley
December, 2004

ACKNOWLEDGMENTS

To Mitch Anthony and Advisor Insights Press, without whose support this book would not have been possible.

To Bobbye Middendorf, a gifted writer and editor, who transformed my manuscripts into far more readable and effective work.

To my colleagues; it is always a pleasure working with professionals.

To the many who have attended my seminars, read my articles, and commented, questioned, criticized, and praised—I've learned much from you, thank you.

THE WINDS OF CHANGE

I would like to tell you a story about the future of retirement. You will have to decide if the story sounds plausible to you. If it does, you will then need to decide the impact it will have on you and your clients.

Specifically in this section, we will examine: *what are the trends shaping the workplace, retirement, and old age?*

In a sense, I'm assuming the role of a "futurist"—not someone who predicts the future but rather someone who looks at the relevant data and developing trends and projects them outward, just like a meteorologist will predict what the weather will be like tomorrow, the day after, or next week, based on prevailing weather patterns. So, as a "financial futurist," I will help you preview some of the trends shaping workplaces, retirement, pensions, and how you can position yourself as "Chief Retirement Officer" (CRO) for your clients.

For the last 25 years, the American economy has been moving from large-scale production toward constant innovation. Technology has been the driving force. It has become the basic commodity of a global market in finding, transmitting, using, and organizing knowledge—growing from the convergence of increases in computer power, connectivity, and powerful software. It is now easier for all buyers (especially businesses) to compare, shop, and get better deals. Technology has broadened choices, with increased competition among sellers, thereby enhancing innovation. All companies must improve by adding value or by cutting costs. Enhanced innovation and improved productivity result in better, faster, cheaper products and services. Improved productivity and intensified competition at all levels force every seller to add value and cut costs.

Even profitable companies have eliminated or reduced health benefits, changed pension contributions, and outsourced work to lower wage firms or countries. "Downsizing," "rightsizing," "reengineering," or whatever is the current popular term for firing workers, is now a standard part of corporate strategy.

Who's to blame for all this? Some may blame greedy, evil

corporations, but as products and services become better, faster, and cheaper, competition increases. As consumers, we are reaping the benefits. The American economy has grown, resulting in lower unemployment rates, and productivity has increased without inflation. This is the "creative destruction" described by the economist Schumpeter.[1]

In terms of material quality of life—what we get for our money—most are better off than before. I have a phone in my pocket that can connect to any number, anywhere in the world. One day I dropped my three-year-old phone. When I brought the phone in for repair, they just gave me a new one. "It's cheaper to give you a new one than to repair the old one," remarked the kid behind the counter. "Besides, this one has cooler features."

We could not reap the benefits of the new economy without also experiencing these changes. They are two sides of the same coin. As technology gives buyers more choice and easier ability to switch, it makes sellers less secure. Work is not like it used to be. Everything is becoming more volatile and less predictable.[2]

From one perspective, the statistics present a half-empty glass: bankruptcies in major industries like the steel industry leave retirees holding the bag. Restructured workplaces mean jobs are gone for good, and layoffs are a permanent feature of the cycle. Social Security remains insecure. Early retirement and longer life spans are adding decades to the time that people have to plan for—and fund.

Of course, from another perspective, the glass is half-full. People are living longer and healthier lives. Second, or downshifted, careers give people productive time while increasing their incomes. Retirement accounts are increasingly portable. The wealth of an entire nation will be given to the participants. There are opportunities for financial advisors to act now to shape a book of business that will serve them and their clients well into this uncertain future.

Still, the traditional three-legged stool of retirement—pensions, Social Security, and personal funds—for many now teeters precariously. Meanwhile, fluctuations in the stock market have drastically changed the picture for those who did sock away money in retirement funds, with some people seeing dramatic loss of paper profits. Workers' stories consist of confusion, despair, and anger that their retirement expectations have to change. The workplace as we've known it is in flux.

Consider the hurricane. When a hurricane is brewing far out in the ocean, meteorologists study its trajectory and measure rainfall and wind speeds. But even with the most sophisticated equipment, they don't know how powerful the storm will be by the time it hits landfall, nor are they completely certain where it will hit. They deal in probabilities. Based on those probabilities, the Weather Service issues warnings to communities in the (likely) line of the storm.

If a major storm is headed your way, consider the options. Some people stay put, determined to ride it out. They buy provisions, batteries, and flashlights, board up the windows, and fill sandbags to hold back floods. Others prepare to evacuate, packing necessities, and perhaps also boarding up the windows. They might make hotel reservations or move in with family out of harm's way instead of stocking up to ride out the storm. Both are taking steps to prepare, as well as to protect themselves, their loved ones, and their property to get through the storm as safely as possible—albeit in different ways.

That they make preparations and take precautions in the face of a storm is considered a wise move. Those who do nothing might be considered foolhardy. What about the financial storms brewing just off the radar? Some are willing to face the looming trends and probabilities. As a "financial futurist," I can outline strategies to prepare yourself, your business, and your clients using the tools at hand.

Or, to use another example, knowing El Niño is coming every seven or so years doesn't mean you can stop it...*but you can prepare for its effects*.

As financial advisor, you can do the same thing with the retirement plans of your clients. Exploring and understanding the forces shaping the future of retirement doesn't mean you can predict it specifically or change its outcome, but merely that you can prepare for it. Still, that preparation can mean additional assets for your business and a solid financial plan for your clients. You can play a pivotal role in your clients' lives when these storms hit.

First, though, you have to become aware of the prevailing weather patterns we face when it comes to pensions, the workplace, structural unemployment, and the financial readiness (or lack thereof) for the largest cohort of people ever to hit retirement at one time. The 76 million Baby Boomers will shift the meaning of retirement, working, old age, and everything else—just as this population bulge has reshaped every other life stage.

I will give you a tour of what is likely to happen as together we survey and summarize the prevailing trends. There's a high probability of the equivalent of a hurricane on the horizon in the lives of your clients. *The Winds of Change* are blowing. Now is the time to help your clients prepare for the stormy weather ahead.

Chapter 1

THE IMPENDING PENSION CRISIS

Work isn't like it used to be. Jobs aren't guaranteed for life, and neither are pensions. Just ask anyone in the steel industry—where dozens of companies filed for Chapter 11 bankruptcy just in the past five years. Going bankrupt, the companies leave their pension obligations to be covered by the Pension Benefit Guaranty Corporation (PBGC). Other potentially troubled industries include automakers and airlines, but none are immune.

Generous pensions and health care benefits, called "legacy costs," for an ever-increasing pool of retired workers are considered to be among the culprits pushing some corporations into bankruptcy. The impending pension crisis will continue the wake-up call for workers as well as for companies. People are learning that they have to be responsible for their own retirements. This trend puts you as a financial advisor in the position of helping guide working people through the retirement decision-making process.

Underfunded

Pensions, one leg of the three-legged stool of funding retirement, are in big trouble. Pension funds, the monies corporations have promised to put away for the retirement of workers and current retirees, are underfunded by some estimates approaching $300 billion. According to research from Greenwich Associates, assets of corporate pension plans have lost $500 billion in value over the past few years.[1] Companies don't have enough money to pay for their commitments.

Even the Government Accounting Office (GAO) recently indicated there's a pension crisis. There are many reasons for the problems—none of them good—

especially if you're at the wrong end of the pension check. The equities in pension funds for workers and retirees took a hit along with the rest of the stock market over the past few years. For companies who had these defined benefit assets in short-term, fixed-income securities, their funds suffered poor results with the lower interest rates. Questionable accounting practices have taken their toll on pensions as well. Senior executives who take care of their own retirement through golden parachutes have no qualms about positioning workers' retirement benefits as liabilities to be shed through bankruptcy, mergers or converting conventional pensions to "cash balance" plans. Commentators like *Business Week* columnist Robert Kuttner go so far as to call it "The Great American Pension-Fund Robbery."[3]

> *"A pension crisis threatens the solvency of American corporations, cities, and states, and even the federal government."[2]*
>
> *–Ronald J. Ryan and Frank J. Fabozzi*
> *The Journal of Investing*

In 1974, the Employee Retirement Income Security Act (ERISA) classified underfunding of defined benefit plans. If the market value of assets in a plan falls below 90 percent of its current liabilities, such deficits must be resolved (funded) within five years.[4] This is the reason that General Motors (GM) recently issued bonds for $17 billion—to meet their funding requirement. More about GM and its headaches a little later.

In the final quarter of 2002, Merrill Lynch announced that 98 percent of the 346 S&P 500 companies who did have defined benefit pension plans would be underfunded by year-end.[5] For 2003, Credit Suisse First Boston reported that pension obligations continue to rise, meaning more companies are underfunded this year than last in spite of an improvement in stock values.[6]

Who Has a Pension?

But who has a pension any more anyway? Haven't they all been replaced with 401(k)s and other defined contribution plans? It's true. A growing number of workers don't have to worry about pensions. Currently just 16 percent of employees are covered by pensions, down from the 1975 Labor Department figures indicating there were 29 percent of workers who named guaranteed benefit pensions as their primary retirement plan. Still, according to Kuttner, 42 million workers and retirees with assets reaching $1.6 trillion dollars are still in traditional pension plans.[7]

Typically, the largest companies are the most likely to have pension plans for workers. Now, rating agencies like S & P and Moody's are looking at unfunded pension liabilities as debt, much to the consternation of the companies. The cost of their own retirees is simply too much for companies to maintain.

Frank's Experience with Big Steel

Frank worked in the steel industry all his life and at his last company for more than 30 years. With his wife Mary, a teacher, he raised a family, and looked forward to a comfortable retirement, complete with health insurance, and time to finally do all the things he never had the time to do. Over the years, he and fellow steelworkers went on strike now and then for better wages or benefits. A few times, the concessions included improved retirement benefits. Finally, he'd get to take advantage of all that.

Frank retired a few years ago. He and Mary traveled in their RV, often driving out of the midwestern city they called home just as winter started blowing in. Last year, Frank and Mary heard that Frank's company was filing for bankruptcy. What would happen to Frank's expected monthly pension check of $1,768.42 from the steel company? They got an unpleasant surprise when they learned that a company in bankruptcy does not pay its retirees—neither pension nor health insurance benefit, a situation that concerns them. Though they have some savings plus Mary's pension from the state and a 403(b), they are looking for someone to help explain a letter they received saying that they would be receiving $1,424.56 from someone they'd never heard of—the PBGC. Frank doesn't understand why his house is worth five times what he paid for it, why the school district is trying to lure Mary back from retirement with a DROP plan, or why his pension plan is going down.

PBGC to the Rescue

Frank will continue to receive a portion of his pension, although a lesser amount than he expected, courtesy of the quasi-governmental agency, the Pension Benefit Guaranty Corporation. The PBGC insures the basic benefits of 44 million American workers with pensions in the approximately 32,500 private defined benefit plans.[8] Unfortunately, it doesn't guarantee the full amount. Every private defined benefit plan must have the plan approved by the IRS and pay a membership fee to the PBGC as backup insurance should some of the pension programs fail (i.e., their companies go bankrupt). The PBGC and its membership fees were also part of the ERISA rules. What foresight—all the way back in 1974!

At least Frank is getting in early. In fact, another potentially ticking time bomb is the PBGC itself. In May 2003, according to *The Economist*, in its special report on corporate pensions, the PBGC went from a surplus of $7.7 billion to a deficit of $5.4 billion in a matter of months.[9] The PBGC has taken on the pension obligations of 30 bankrupt steel companies and several troubled airlines on top of billions of other dollars over the past few years. At the same time, this fund has suffered from low interest rates and market losses, along with everyone else. A year and a half after the *Economist* report, PBGC's deficit continues to ballon, with late 2004 figures indicating dramatic funding shortfalls. PBGC's long-term liabilities are clocking in 60 percent higher than available assets (see sidebar).

"While the PBGC's $39 billion in assets would enable it to meet its obligations for a few years, they can only go so far in funding its $62 billion liability."[10]

–David M. Katz, CFO.com

If the PBGC continues to undertake the pension obligations of increasing numbers of failing companies, it will be unable to remain solvent. Of course the government cannot let all these pensions go up in smoke. Remember the S&L bailout? The PBGC is potentially the next in line for a massive taxpayer-funded bailout.

The Legacy of Big Steel

Since we're taking a "financial futurist" perspective, it's useful to review the path of one industry that is radically reshaping itself. From there, we can then identify other potential problem areas.

When the steel industry faced its initial challenges from foreign manufacturers, waves of worker layoffs hit the industry. These layoffs started the pronounced skewing of non-working to active steelworkers that continues to plague the industry. For all organizations that provide lifetime benefits, it's a growing problem, and it's called "legacy costs." It's the legacy they receive, including pension, health benefits, life insurance, and dependent coverage.

Much ink has been spilled over the steel industry. There's plenty of blame and finger-pointing on both sides. Some accuse the unions of being greedy. Others accuse the companies of reneging on a commitment to American workers who powered our economy during the second half of the last century. Meanwhile, foreign competitors came in and ate our lunch—along with breakfast and dinner.

According to *The Wall Street Journal* writer Robert Guy Matthews, the steel industry's current painful transformation has a great deal to do with its long-promised obligations to its retirees. Because retirees from this beleaguered industry outnumber current workers, it looks like the classic scene that has been painted

time and again about Social Security—not enough people paying in to cover
for the ones who are still collecting. Matthews indicates that the tab for big
steel's past promises to retirees for life and health insurance and pensions is
$10 billion.[11]

As steel companies grapple with liquidating—leaving retirees and their
dependents without promised benefits—the steel unions are working to figure out
whether they can keep some U.S. jobs in the industry by making concessions on
retiree benefits in an industry that has lost jobs to overseas firms for many years.

Years ago, when hundreds of thousands of jobs in the steel industry paid well
and its unions were among the strongest in the nation, strikes were often settled
by enriching future benefits, since the steel companies often felt too strapped to
pay more in the present term. They shifted their commitments to retirement, into
the future. This is the legacy that they are dealing with now. That largess has all
but evaporated.

The Pension Crisis Affects Spouses Too

*Janet is the surviving spouse of steelworker Tom who died in 1990.
She is dependent on the pension she continues to receive and is grateful
for the health coverage that helps her afford needed medication for high
blood pressure and several other health problems. Janet will suffer when
her husband's company declares bankruptcy and can no longer pay
health coverage and pension benefits. What will Janet do?*

There are no easy answers. According to steelworker union information,
600,000 retired steel workers and their families receive health care benefits from a
steel company. Lawmakers have introduced controversial legislation to help
address steel industry legacy costs, without success. Critics point out that other
industries are also grappling with this issue, and favoring one industry with taxpayer support would be unfair. According to United
Auto Workers' President Ron Gettelfinger in a speech
before the Detroit Economic Club, "A lot of people are
curious to know how we're going to solve the problem
of rising health care. We're not. You can't fix the
health care crisis at any one bargaining table."[12]

While the steel industry restructures, another solution has been put forward. Distressed asset investor
Wilbur Ross, who purchased assets of the former LTV

> *"Half of all workers have no
> pension at work, but those that
> do are up against companies
> bailing out of guaranteed pen-
> sions while cutting retirement
> contributions."[13]*
>
> *–Robert Borosage, TomPaine.com*

Steel (now called International Steel Group), "does agree to put money aside in a fund that can be drawn by retired workers who need help with medical expenses."[14]

Who's Next?

Trend-watchers see the airline industry as another potential trouble spot. US Airways has declared bankruptcy for the second time. United Airlines wants to discontinue funding its $13 billion pension plan while the company remains in bankruptcy. Their request should trouble you. If the PBGC takes over United Airlines' plan obligations, watch for the domino effect throughout the airline industry. If the government guarantees an industry's liability, that liability will be shifted to the government. Already, bankruptcies have sent some airline pension funds to be covered by the PBGC. Some of us see these problems wherever we look.

I'm based near Chicago, so consider Figure 1.1 below of the Chicago region's largest employers, a list of venerable institutions. These bastions of a

FIGURE 1.1	Rethinking Work 15 Largest Employers in Chicago[15]		
EMPLOYER	**NUMBER OF WORKERS**		**LAYOFF RISK**
1. U.S. GOVERNMENT	75,000		PROBABLE
2. CHICAGO PUBLIC SCHOOLS	46,179		POSSIBLE
3. CITY OF CHICAGO	40,324		DEFINITE
4. JEWEL-OSCO	39,201		POSSIBLE
5. COOK COUNTY	27,042		DEFINITE
6. SBC AMERITECH	22,400		DEFINITE
7. ADVOCATE HEALTH CARE	20,573		POSSIBLE
8. UNITED PARCEL SERVICE	19,373		POSSIBLE
9. STATE OF ILLINOIS	18,915		DEFINITE
10. UNITED AIRLINES	18,276		DEFINITE
11. MOTOROLA	18,000		DEFINITE
12. ARCHDIOCESE OF CHICAGO	17,964		PROBABLE
13. ABBOTT LABORATORIES	17,333		POSSIBLE
14. TARGET CORP	16,300		POSSIBLE
15. WALGREENS	14,743		POSSIBLE

Information from Crain's Chicago Business

conservative, stable labor force have been around for decades, centuries even! Now look again. What do you think are the potential risks for these thousands of employees to lose their jobs? You can make your own list of the top 10 or 15 employers in your area. In most cases, their workers will look just as vulnerable.

What Drives the Auto Industry

As one of the cornerstone companies in the US economy, it used to be said, "What's good for GM is good for the nation." Now, a more sobering perspective might be, "What's worrying GM probably ought to worry the nation." As the biggest of the Big-Three automakers, it's that pesky legacy cost business all over again, written so large we'll be sure to see it.

At present, General Motors has 460,000 retirees. For comparison, that's roughly the size of the entire U.S. Army.[16] In contrast, Ford has only 130,000 retirees. GM has *2.5 retirees for every active worker*, while Ford's and Chrysler's ratios are more manageable at 1:1. They went through painful layoffs and downsizing several years ago when GM was still going strong.

The pension and health care bills related to these retirees are enormous. GM spent over $1 billion in medical and insurance costs for its retirees in 2002. Over the next 13 years, this figure is expected to top out at a staggering $38 billion. Quite a legacy at GM.

Pension-wise, GM is facing a huge cash-flow crisis. At the end of 2001, GM's pension plan assets were short approximately $9 billion. The continued drop in the stock market leads analysts to believe that the unfunded portion could total almost $20 billion in the very near future. Under current regulations, GM must fund the pension shortfall, plowing an estimated $2.2 billion into the fund throughout 2002.

Recently GM issued $17 billion worth of bonds, just to maintain their retirement funding requirement. This is not money that will be used in improved plants and equipment. It won't streamline their processes. It's going into their pension plan. Such actions bring on the pundits: "GM manages pension assets, provides health care — and even makes cars," says Roger Lowenstein in *Smart Money*. He indicates that the company spends more on health care per car than on steel, claiming "both GM's asset-management business and its in-house 'health maintenance organization' are bigger than

> *"At 109, Earnest Pusey is the oldest of GM's centenarians. "He is one of 240 GM retirees or spouses over 100-years-old. All of them are older than GM itself, which is four years from its centennial ... The projected cost of providing health care benefits to current and future retirees like Mr. Pusey is a staggering $63 billion."[17]*
>
> *–Danny Hakim, New York Times*

its vehicle business."[18] So, in addition to worrying about all the issues of a major manufacturer, GM adds the headaches caused by taking on the roles of money manager and health care organization.

In more graphic terms, GM's combined annual pension, insurance, and medical costs for these retirees ate up $900 for every vehicle it sold in 2002—a figure that is expected to rise to $1,300 by 2005. Or, consider that for every GM retiree, the company sells just 14 vehicles.[19]

At number two, automaker Ford, health care costs run about $2 billion per year for 640,000 US employees, retirees, and dependents. That's a price tag higher than what it spends on steel in any given year.[20]

The Winds of Change Begin to Blow

The impending pension crisis is now upon us. Too many companies are having trouble funding pensions, and legacy costs including health care have gone through the roof. These problems are the tip of an iceberg in the coming dramatic shift in the way we work, as we'll discuss this in more detail in the next chapter. For some entire industries, these high costs have forced dramatic changes, with mergers, layoffs, downsizing, structural unemployment, and reengineering the norm.

Other companies, even without the specific problems of pensions and health-care costs, have been choosing the rightsizing route, shedding workers as they go. The workers are left to pick up the pieces, decide the next step in their work and lives, and try to sort out the finances both for now and later. As a financial advisor, you have the tools to help them make the decisions to see them through a life-long journey.

As *The Winds of Change* accelerate to hurricane speed, workers face numerous imposing developments in the workplace. As CRO, this is the opportunity for you to sit down with your clients and help them structure their finances—and their lives. You can help them address the basics of financial planning while identifying and developing alternative income streams to see them through future changes. Even as traditional pensions and company-funded retirement accounts diminish, we are also seeing a dramatic shift in employment patterns. As we discuss in the next chapter, the coming "free-agent nation," forming as a result of structural unemployment, holds both opportunities and perils. Like preparations before a storm, your critical one-on-one work with clients will help them meet the "structural unemployment challenges" and whatever else develops in the workplace or in society at large.

Chapter 2

STRUCTURAL UNEMPLOYMENT

For the last 25 years or so, America has been moving from a stable, large-scale production economy to one of continuous innovation. The fundamental change of this "creative destruction" has had a chilling effect on the social programs our country has in place.

In July 2003, *The Wall Street Journal* reported the number of jobless hit a 20-year high.[1]

Long-term economic shifts combined with major changes in markets can result in unemployment that lasts a long time as whole classes of jobs disappear. In many cases, without retraining, the unemployed can end up without work permanently. This is in stark contrast to what we experienced—and what our safety net systems of unemployment insurance were designed to address over the past half-century—when cyclical unemployment was the norm.

Growing up with cyclical unemployment meant that factories might close for a few weeks, up to a few months to retool. Workers would be temporarily laid off, could collect unemployment insurance to help make ends meet, then could generally count on being called back once the improvements and upgrades on the line were complete. In other cases, the layoffs were due to seasonal fluctuations in the need for the products. Either way, the safety net available (time-limited, government-sponsored unemployment insurance) was created to fit this specific pattern of temporary unemployment. Even COBRA and vesting rules hearken back to a different world of work.

The Diversity of Structural Changes

The safety net of unemployment insurance was certainly not created for structural unemployment—what we're living through now.

As the manufacturing base shifts to technology and subsequently to a service focus, some factories close their doors permanently; unable to compete, products obsolete. Some jobs, even technological support positions, are migrating to cheaper labor overseas. Other employers continue to need the work done, but can't afford employees with costly benefits, pensions, and retirement packages. They often restructure the work force using temporary labor. Sometimes layoffs come in anticipation of a company being acquired, and so the balance sheet looks better. If layoffs don't come before, then count on them once the acquisition is complete.

> *"We have been in the longest stretch of manufacturing retrenchment in post-World War II history."[2]*
>
> *–Jon E. Hilsenrath,*
> *The Wall Street Journal*

Other industries like steel, as discussed in the prior chapter, reorganize through bankruptcy. Every company is constantly reviewing all lines of business, poised to close down any units that don't meet financial benchmarks. Structural unemployment means that seismic economic shifts leave no jobs or far fewer jobs, less well-paying jobs, or jobs without benefits, where many well-paying, full-time jobs with benefits used to be. And it's not just Rust Belt workers who are affected. A recent *Fast Company* story reported that even "Big Blue" is outsourcing to overseas workers.[3]

No matter how the restructuring happens, most workers today are discovering that the rule of thumb is for every $10,000 in income, it will take at least one month to find a job. Count on a minimum of six months to find work for the $60,000 worker; ten months for the $100,000 worker. That time-frame is for workers whose skills are still sharp and needed in the current economy. The downsized, right-sized, reengineered, just-in-time layoff can happen when workers reach 35 . . . or 45 . . . or 55, and almost

> *"The Labor Department said that 22 percent of all unemployed workers have been out of work for more than half a year, the highest ratio of long-term unemployed workers since 1992."[4]*
>
> *–The Wall Street Journal*

always through no fault of their own. In fact, it's as often the top producer (hence, the most expensive person on the payroll) as it is a lower level worker. Usually it's both.

Bob's Story: A Lifetime at the Phone Company

Bob, age 54, worked for the phone company since getting out of college. He likes to say he started at the phone company but now he works for a wholly owned subsidiary of a fully integrated communications network company. The company has split once, been merged twice, and recently was bought. Bob keeps a collection of golf shirts with the different logos of the ever-changing business. What worries Bob now is what he and his coworkers call "package time." The package doesn't worry Bob; what concerns him is how will he make it to 59 1/2—when he can get all of his money penalty-free from the retirement plan.

"Offshoring"

At least Bob hasn't encountered the "offshoring" phenomenon. As an adjective turned into a verb, it's pretty ugly. Plan on hearing that term a lot. For those losing jobs to foreign workers, it's a painful recognition that there's a global marketplace and companies are only too happy to move jobs where labor is cheapest. In fact, some venture capital firms won't even consider funding a company unless there's some kind of plan in place for using less expensive offshore workers to bring innovative technological projects to market.[5]

According to Forrester Research, over the next 15 years, more than three million US service industry jobs and up to $136 billion in wages will move overseas.[6] What's the savings rate? By some counts, work can get done at 1/5 the cost using offshore employees.

For years, Hawn reports, IBM has been sending coding work abroad.[7] A December, 2003 *The Wall Street Journal* report indicated that up to 4,730 engineering and management jobs are now moving offshore—making white-collar, middle-class jobs next in line.[8] Gartner, Inc. views the end of 2004 as the time for one out of every ten jobs in the computer software industry to move abroad.[9]

In another report, researchers at Fisher Center for Real Estate and Urban Economics at the University of California, Berkeley point out that potentially 14 million service jobs are on the line.[10] *Translation:* 11 percent of the nation's jobs are vulnerable to being sent offshore.

Economic Outlook Headline: "Outsourcing abroad draws debate at home."[11]

–Headline from The Wall Street Journal

Temping It

What happens when companies face the untenable position of still needing workers to do the work but can no longer afford the added load of benefits, pensions, and funding retirement accounts? In the case of many large (generally non-union) employers, companies often go through a dramatic restructuring. Instead of employees with costly benefits, pensions, and retirement packages, what if they could get the same people to do the work without these extras? This kind of restructuring turns employees into temps, often using a newly formed in-house "temp agency" to hire people back.

Even while the company has a huge layoff, simultaneously many of the laid-off workers are rehired back at their old jobs—maybe even at the same desks—but through a temporary agency, and without benefits. At first, it might seem like a good deal to employees. Usually they receive some kind of severance package. As they get "rehired" as temps, they sometimes receive higher pay as temporary or contract workers than they received as salary. As temporary workers, they are also technically able to take a day off if desired—without pay, of course.

"Census sees a surge in Americans without insurance: No health coverage for 43.6 million as employer-based plans shrink."[12]

—Headline in The Wall Street Journal

Will the temp pay be sufficient to cover taxes as an independent contractor and pay for health, life, and disability insurance? How many of those newly created temp workers are prepared to fund their own retirement accounts with that "extra" pay? Workers who envision taking a short week as a temp are in for a rude awakening. The seeming flexibility of calling your own hours evaporates with the realities of how far that temp paycheck *doesn't* stretch. Many workers find they need a second or even third job on top of their former, now restructured job, just to make up the cost of lost salary and benefits.

We've been through jobless recoveries. We've been through recoveries where hundreds of thousands of new jobs have been created. But if it takes three of those newly created jobs to make up for the one job you used to have, what's that supposed to mean?

Jason's Story: Even the Tech-Savvy Aren't Immune

Jason was one of the eager young tech workers during the dotcom craze. While he wasn't a high-flying owner, he was positioning himself for a bright future. The company had a 401(k), but it was the stock options that Jason thought would make him rich. His skills were second to none, and he could work at his projects for hours on end. After the bubble burst, the company laid him off. The stock options were worthless. He hasn't looked at his 401(k). Jason turned to contract or project work. He has been working steadily, and the money is good, but what worries him is the unpredictability of the future. He would like to save for retirement, but he is independent. There is no company 401(k).

The Evolution of the Nation's Leading Employer

In 1970, the country's largest private employer was a manufacturer, General Motors, with 350,000 workers. Overwhelmingly union, workers earned $17.50 an hour plus health, pension, vacation benefits, and cost-of-living increases. Today, the country's largest private employer is the retail giant Wal-Mart, with over one million U.S. workers. Wal-Mart workers earn an average hourly wage of $8.00, with no defined benefit pension and inadequate health care.[13]

Yet, even that pales in comparison with the two million people per day who are employed by staffing companies. Today, temporary services dominate the private employer market. These are working people not defined as employees and lacking retirement plans and benefits.[14]

Bankruptcies and Airline Industry Turbulence

As discussed earlier, industries like steel have seen many of their companies reorganizing through bankruptcy. They restructure with far fewer jobs, often without the benefits or pensions that former workers received. The industry continues, but the workers are in a far different position financially. The troubled airlines seem to be following in the steel industry's footsteps.

Airlines are also more familiar in everyday awareness. Many more people have experienced the ambience of an airplane than have experienced the excitement of a steel mill. While much goes on behind the scenes, airlines include a lot of front-line service people, unlike the steel industry. Will the carriers be able to bounce back from bankruptcy with unhappy employees interacting with customers, serving drinks, and selling tickets?

Due to bankruptcies (or airlines trying desperately to sidestep bankruptcy), most airline workers report significant pay cuts and givebacks to their companies, fueling dispirited attitudes, according to Wendy Zellner, reporting in *Business Week*. She profiles the challenges of airline personnel at the top three companies

(See Figure 2.1). A pilot experiences a 31 percent salary cut as well as a demotion from captain to first officer; the mechanic, a 13 percent drop in hourly pay; and a couple, both flight attendants, each end up working three extra days per month as they scramble to arrange schedules so someone is always at home with the kids. While these people aren't out of a job yet, their work lives and finances have been dramatically rearranged. According to Zellner, many airline workers are looking at 2008 before their pay is back up to where it was.[15]

FIGURE 2.1	**Reducing Headcounts** Cutting to the Bone[16]	
	Head count reduction*	**Annual Payroll Drop***
American	13,200 or 13%	$1.8 billion or 23%
United	17,200 or 20%	$2.6 billion or 25%
US Airways	6,700 or 19%	$1.2 billion or 25%

Since 2002 — Data: BusinessWeek

Acquisitions

Mergers and acquisitions continue to change the makeup of employers in the workplace. Not only are smaller companies being acquired by larger companies, but large companies are also being acquired by still larger companies. Within any of those companies, there are business units that don't "fit" with the stated business goals. So, a constant flux of buying and selling companies and business units as well as restructuring departments keeps everyone dancing.

Workers can expect layoffs both in anticipation of a company being acquired (that way, the balance sheet looks better), as well as after. Post-merger, people handling duplicate functions are called "redundancies." For those who happen to survive the pre-acquisition layoffs, count on still more changes once the acquisition is complete.

It's Nothing Personal—Tom's Story: Part One

Structural unemployment can happen to anyone, and through no fault of one's own. It happened to me—twice. The second time, I could have kicked myself for not seeing it coming. Here's what happened.

The first time, I was the senior person and supervisor on a financial service firm's customer telephone Help Desk. Our group consisted of five people: an assistant and four of us on the phones. As the most experienced person on the desk, I could address nearly every financial query that came along. ("Give Tom the calls where the deceased forgot to change the beneficiary from his first wife to the second." "Give him the odd, the technical, the challenging.")

As the firm's owners came around asking about what we all did, I felt pretty confident. The new assistant couldn't answer any of the customers' questions. The remaining members of the Help Desk team each had background in one particular product type. No one had comprehensive background in all aspects of the financial products we sold. I knew I'd be the one they'd keep—just so they could continue to run the Help Desk efficiently.

What I hadn't counted on was that because of my depth of experience, I was also the highest paid person on the desk. As the owners were "cleaning up" the balance sheet in preparation for selling the company, they were looking for high-ticket salaries that they could dispense with. That happened to include my salary. They could continue to run the desk with the less expensive people. Once they sold the company, the new firm would have its own Help Desk staff. In all likelihood, my colleagues would not last long past the final acquisition.

I was let go and went through a grieving process, including several months of anger and questioning, "What did I do wrong?" Every way I looked at it, no suitable answer came to mind. In fact, I'd done nothing wrong. It was purely a business decision. I just happened to be the guy with the salary they needed to cut.

Just a Business Decision

It's a short step from acquisitions and mergers to closing down a business unit because it is underperforming or because it no longer fits in the company's chosen strategic direction. Because all work is taking place at high speed, and companies live or die on quarterly profitability, decisions that once took years are now made

EBRI reported on the US Census Bureau's Current Population Survey (CPS). In 2002, it showed "the median tenure for male wage and salary workers declined from 5.9 years in 1983 to 4.0 years in 2002."[17]

–EBRI.org

in seemingly split-second increments.

Some outsider who doesn't know anyone at the company can come in and make a dispassionate business decision. Generally, these outsiders are consultants, or even "the numbers guy from another region." They have no connection with the actual people being put out of work. They can come in, look at the numbers, and make the decision. After being let go from the company preparing for acquisition, I became a member of the unit that was suddenly no longer part of the business! Following that second ouster, I later became that outsider who came in, looked at the numbers, and told them how to downsize to get out of a line of business that wasn't a fit with their core ventures. I know all about it. I've been on both sides of the desk.

It's (Still) Nothing Personal—Tom's Story: Part Two

Eventually, I landed a job at another financial services firm. I worked hard for three years or so selling retirement plans. In fact, I was their top producer in selling the 401(k) line. Despite all my hard work, I realized all was not well with the company's 401(k) retirement unit. My colleagues and I joked about the possibility of not having a place to call work. I said, "You know, they're going to close this unit." That was maybe a week before everyone was called to a meeting. We were asked to bring our laptops for an upgrade. Instead, we turned them in as the unit was shut down. So, my one-week warning came to pass. I was angry. This time, there wasn't even time to save the contacts list on my computer. Mostly, I was angry with myself for not realizing this was coming sooner and making better preparations.

Now, at my current employer, I'm the guy who can help the managers in a distant city close down the underperforming business line. I don't know the people. It's just a business decision.

Advisor Opportunities Arising from Structural Unemployment

Welcome to the ever-changing world of structural unemployment. Once again, in this brave new workplace, people must take personal responsibility for their financial futures. They can no longer expect to be in one job, or even one industry, for an entire working lifetime. Now they must retool themselves and upgrade their skills constantly to meet all-new challenges in the workplace.

When the inevitable changes strike, to whom will your clients turn? Even if it is "just a business decision," such workplace changes have a profound effect on the people involved. Will your clients know what to do? Will you be able to guide them through the stresses of their financial decisions?

Clients will need your insights now more than ever. With your help, they will learn what to do to become more self-reliant when it comes to the issues surrounding retirement. By understanding the effects of structural unemployment on the majority of those in the workforce—no matter what the color of their collars—you will be positioning yourself as the "tour guide" in this strange new terrain.

Workers can be let go after two years, five years, ten years, or 30 years. It may be due to bankruptcy, acquisition, downsizing, offshoring, or obsolescence. Whatever the reason, it means starting over at 35 or at 55. The traditional concept of work, with a tenure of 35 years and a gold watch on retirement, just doesn't exist anymore. With the huge number of part-time workers, consultants, temporaries, and contract workers replacing full-time, benefit-eligible employees, it won't exist in the future either. Therein lies the opportunity for *rethinking work* that we will focus on next.

Chapter 3

RETHINKING WORK

"We live in a society that still largely represents retirement as an ultimatum. Either you work or you retire. This ultimatum is foolish, counter-intuitive, and counterproductive for the good of society...Once we find work we really enjoy, the payoff becomes more than the paycheck. Why walk away from a meaningful payoff if you don't need to? As people age, they must be careful to not confuse the desire to cut back on working hours with the choice to retire altogether."[1]
  - *Mitch Anthony, Author*

They say the Chinese character for "danger" can also be read as "opportunity." You can see the glass as half-empty—or half-full. For financial advisors, these workplace changes mean money in motion, opportunities to become the trusted advisor for your clients as you help them navigate the many work-life and financial-life changes.

Structural unemployment and the pension crisis are the inevitable results of the dramatic technological innovations driving the impersonal process of creative destruction. While change is required so society does not stagnate, it now seems like the change process is on steroids. Still, there's no going back. Like the weather, it's inevitable. We can either prepare—or not. It's not all bleak, though. There are new opportunities both for those whose work lives are shifting, as well as for those who choose to advise them. The fast and furious pace of change caused by technology includes increased competitive pressures, a

Estimates from Spectrem Group show more than $3.7 trillion will exit from qualified retirement plans of all types by mid-decade, over $450 billion of that amount occurred in 2002 alone.[2]

-Spectrum Group

requirement for constant innovation, and "better, cheaper, faster" products to address consumer demands. According to statistics from the Department of Labor, at the end of 2000, people were changing jobs on average once every four years. Such turbulence can be transformed into opportunities as companies continue to seek talented people, whether employees or contingent workers. Meanwhile, there's a growing population of people who have a great deal of work experience, and who are approaching what has historically been thought of as retirement age. The 77 million (give or take) Baby Boomers born between 1946 and 1964 are changing the meanings of work, retirement, and old age, even as work itself is changing.

Legacy Costs Versus Demographic Needs: What's an Employer to Do?

Companies are facing an interesting conundrum that is likely just to get more pronounced. While many corporations are offering early retirement packages to older or long-term workers, other organizations, equally concerned with creating a healthy balance sheet, realize the situation is more complex than mere cost cutting. These employers are also aware that as an aging workforce approaches retirement age, they take with them all kinds of knowledge and experience that isn't readily available elsewhere in the organization. These companies are becoming concerned about the potential "brain drain." If all the experienced employees do take early

retirement, there's a dearth of young people who are prepared to fill the gaps. Consequently, as some companies address their balance sheets by laying off more expensive workers, other organizations are creating savvy ways to keep the wisdom on the payroll—either part-time or by converting employees to temporary workers.

Is it just me or did the power companies all start to get rid of their older workers over the last four or five years? Then, all of a sudden, California seemed to run out of electricity. Why do I see two 20-year-olds at the plant? Heavily tattooed, bodies pierced to the point that they look

FIGURE 3.1

"Dude, we're out of electricity! Call the old guy and see where he used to put it."

like they have been rolled in the tackle box, they are standing at the power plant saying, "Dude, we are out of electricity! Call the old guy and see where he used to put it!" (See Figure 3.1) Author Mitch Anthony writes, "Home Depot announced a national hiring campaign of 'retirees' (coordinated with AARP). The rationale for the campaign? 'They know more and they sell more.' Welcome to the dawning of the Experience Age where gray hair indicates gray matter and the capitalist marketplace realizes the errors of its 'youth-seeking' ways. Home Depot's move is an initial flare in what will become a firestorm of exploiting the commercial value of experience and wisdom. This sort of value doesn't come in 25-year-old containers."[3]

Looking at the workplace demographically, 77 million US Baby Boomers are fast approaching retirement age. Only 45 million 25- to 34-year-olds are lining up behind them. Many companies will need to create solutions. Eventually, the Boomers' kids, a shadow boom, will start to come up to speed in the workplace. Meanwhile, corporations are going to need older workers. They just won't want them as employees.

According to Sandy Aird in *Plan Sponsor*, "At Deloitte Consulting, CEO Doug McCracken saw, as far back as 1998, the potential for organizational brain drain. Deloitte Consulting came up with the firm's *Senior Partners Program* after discovering an estimated 40 percent of its 850 partners will be eligible for benefits from the Deloitte retirement plans in 2003. The phased retirement program offers a solution. It allows partners, age 50 at least, to carve out a second career for themselves within Deloitte, or to work in the same position but at a less hectic pace. Their skills and knowledge are valued; thus, they get to redefine their jobs as part-time, flex-time, different assignments, and shorter projects. This allows the senior partners more time and space for personal fulfillment while Deloitte continues to benefit from having an experienced workforce."[4]

The Redefinition of Work

Over the years, as everything speeded up, people didn't stay in the same company for an entire career. People moved around within their industries, even between industries. Technology salespeople got real estate licenses. Downsized executives became brokers. Consider the words used to describe today's successful worker and workplace: flexible, adaptable, creative, resilient, versatile, and innovative. All of these words involve change. The decision-making skills and attitudes workers need are the willingness to keep an open mind and the ability to be not only comfortable with, but positive about, uncertainty.

Change is occurring more rapidly and events are becoming less predictable in the world of work. Traditional job definitions are morphing into multi-functional roles. Work functions, once defined based on organizational charts, are being fulfilled by teams. Team members are interchangeable. Some are employees, while others may be temps, part-timers, or free agents. The basic structure of the employer-worker relationships is changing.

Employers are focused on generating results, even as the distractions of restructuring, mergers, acquisitions, managing outsourced work, e-commerce, and global marketing compete for their attention. The message to employees is clear: workers are now expected to manage their own careers, determine the next career action steps, be skilled at formulating career moves, and then make the necessary transitions. Even employees are best served by thinking of themselves as contributing to bottom-line results, just as if they were free agents. Current career guides all advise jobholders to take responsibility for the types of projects they work on and the results they generate, thereby building their personal portfolio of workplace results.

These changes will bring about new definitions of a career. All workers face the challenge of making sense of work and career as they reassess a job's meaning in their lives. Some people are choosing to go for fulfillment. Many mid-career changers from the business world and executive ranks are turning around to become teachers, thus becoming the largest source of new talent in the classroom.

The typical new employment path will become a series of successive contracts where relationships with employers become a transaction. This negotiated arrangement lasts only as long as there is a justifiable business-based need for specific work to be done.

Many view this evolving situation with apprehension. Part of the reason is that change seems risky. Staying the same seems safe. However, if change becomes more rapid, more complex, and more unpredictable, then staying the same becomes uncertain and risky. If everything around you is changing, yet you stay the same, you can't be sure what will happen.

Those Flexible Free Agents

Technology has created opportunities to telecommute, work part-time, work off-site, and work on projects as part of a team—work from anywhere there's a laptop and Internet connection. For some companies, it's all about generating results. To some degree, they don't care when or where their people work, just so they generate the required results. Doing more with less is the mantra. This can also mean that one person is expected to do the job that was formerly done by a team of three!

Other industries draw together experts for discrete projects. These free agents come together temporarily, and then disperse when the project is complete. Consider how Hollywood now works. It's right up there on the screen for everyone to see as the credits roll, and roll, and roll.

When everyone was a worker on the studio's payroll, movie credits were brief. In my presentations, I sometimes compare the single screen of credits from *Gone With the Wind* with numerous pages of credits for a contemporary movie like *Metamorphosis: Alien Factor*. The animated movie, *Toy Story*, even created a mini film of outtakes (Don't ask how an animated movie can have outtakes...) to run behind five or so minutes of credits.

Epic films like *Lord of the Rings* are years in the making, crossing continents and demanding long commitments from a vast army of free agents. Such movies are made with hundreds and hundreds of contractors, consultants, and hired hands. The studios don't own anything anymore except their own lots and some moviemaking rights. Everyone is, in essence, a free agent. Even the catering company is listed in the credits. That firm, too, expands for the project by hiring temporary workers. When the project is over and "it's a wrap," everyone shakes hands, gets their listing in the credits, and then goes out to regroup and find the next project.

> *Another growing trend is temporary workers. Today, about a quarter of U.S. workers are free agents—temporary or contract workers, according to staffing firm Kelly Services.[5]*

As the costs of carrying employees become more arduous—health and insurance benefits, training and education, as well as pension and retirement benefits—many more companies, large and small, are going the way of the movie studios. They hire freelancers, free agents, contractual employees, part-timers, and consultants to shave costs. The future of work is going to look a lot like those Hollywood credits that just keep rolling.

Results-Based Pay

Flexible with time or by project is nothing compared to the new flexibility in pay. Everyone acknowledges that entrepreneurs, consultants, and salespeople experience peaks and valleys in income. Now people employed in corporations are increasingly encountering "flexible" pay schedules. This means that they may have a base salary with commissions or results-oriented bonuses based on meeting senior management's criteria. Maybe there's profit sharing at the end of the year if the company meets annual goals.

Flexible pay means variable pay. Few workers would choose to come up on the lower end of that flexibility. Those with good opportunities to maximize their up-side potential work twice as hard to earn all they can—while they can—never knowing how long it will last. (Remember the lesson from the last chapter: workers can be downsized at any time, through no fault of their own. And it's just as likely to be the top performer!) Pay is now tied to results.

Tom's Story—Part Three

In my current job incarnation, I am one of those frenzied workers, going full throttle (and then some) on behalf of my current organization. Part of my business is giving talks, seminars, and workshops to financial advisors. To do this, my company schedules a year of travel to exciting places like Cleveland, Milwaukee, Oakland, Philadelphia, and Raleigh. Often I am on the road three to five days a week. My family sometimes forgets what I look like. I continue at this frenetic pace because I see the college tuition bills looming a few years ahead and my own retirement following shortly thereafter.

Every day I'm responding to the trends I'm talking to you about. I realize this is my opportunity to make the most of that up-side income potential. Advisors should consider such overachievers as prime potential clients. Why? We are so busy maximizing our income that we will pay for advice in almost any sphere—from finances to technology to home maintenance.

The Bridge Job

There's increasing flexibility for older workers as well. My reading of the trends is that every worker between 46 and 56 can expect to be let go from a job sometime during that decade. Some will get great severance packages; some will get so-so packages; a few will get very little. In any case, these are people who are far from feeling ready to retire. What next?

One recent workplace trend is what Employee Benefits Research Institute (EBRI) calls the "bridge job." The bridge job is a job that is expected to last less than ten years, a part-time position or in a field that differs from a worker's original career. EBRI estimates that it will affect one-third to one-half of the Baby

Boom generation. There will be two different types of bridge jobholders: those who need to work and those who want to work.[6]

For those who have a cushion, receiving some kind of severance or lump sum pension benefit, there are suddenly opportunities that open up, allowing them to recreate or reshape their lives for more meaning or more fulfillment, pursuing a calling, or actively supporting community organizations. While some will need to work, whether for benefits or for more income, many others are in a position to choose not to work—but they want to work anyway. Some will create part time ventures, develop their own dream businesses, or bring their skills and expertise to causes they support. Some will move an avocation to center stage as a new source of income.

FIGURE 3.2	**Rethinking Work** Who is being let go?[8]

If your company used **buyouts,** what is the average length of service of those laid off?

1 – 3 years	11.1%
4 – 5 years	5.6%
6 – 10 years	38.9%
> 10 years	44.4%

Source: Institutional Investor, October 2001

Landon's Story: Bridge Job with a Healthy Cushion

Landon was a mid-level executive at one of the major petroleum companies ever since graduating as an engineer more than 25 years ago. His story exemplifies the statistics in Figure 3-2 above: the longer your tenure at a workplace, the greater your chances of being laid off. As one of the "graying" members of the team, he was called in along with a few dozen other 50-something executives. All had climbed the ladder, increasing their salaries to the low six-figures over their many years of service to the company. Imagine Landon's surprise when the package of benefits he received upon departure was in seven-figures. "I never realized I was rich. I really am a millionaire. It's amazing." Of course, there are tax penalties if he takes possession of that money or tries to access it before he's 59 1 / 2. Depending on his readily available reserves, Landon will likely have many opportunities to reshape his work and his life, with a comfortable financial cushion to support him and his family. He's not ready for full-time golf for 30 or more years.

According to the Bureau of Labor Statistics, 12.3 percent of the workforce was age 55 or over in 1990. A 1992 study by Fairfax, Virginia-based consultants Michael Barth, William McNaught, and Philip Rizzi projects that this figure will top 20 percent by 2020.[9]

- Institutional Investor

For a growing number of Americans, retirement is a chance to become an entrepreneur or to turn a hobby into a career. Other retirees are likely to find that, while work isn't part of their plan, they may need to pursue part-time employment to make ends meet. Many investors simply aren't saving enough to fund their retirement. As a result, many people will not be able to afford to retire. This is already happening, and the phenomenon is expected to become more widespread.

Advisor Opportunities Arising from Rethinking Work

Further estimates from Spectrem Group indicate that over $2 trillion, or about 56 percent of those $3.7 trillion in distributions, will be captured in IRA accounts by the end of 2006, with the amount of eligible rollover assets increasing by a double-digit rate each year.[10]

Building client relationships so they seek out your advice during this mid-life downsizing and career change gives you the opportunity and responsibility for pension, retirement plan, or 401(k) rollovers, potentially the "dream big ticket" rollovers over $100,000. That said, there remain abundant opportunities to systematically capture what our industry deems small- and medium-sized accounts.

There are approximately 5.5 million participants that, in aggregate, control about half a trillion dollars of

Advisor Opportunity:
Some firms, with a large percentage of employees older than age 45, are paying the oldest to leave early. As trillions of dollars come out of retirement plans of the many companies offering early retirement, or as workers job-hop, realize that in any given year, a large percentage of your client base could be eligible for a rollover.

-Financial Research Corporation

401(k) assets. Thus, there are high-balance rollover opportunities to be had. In addition, greater job mobility means that many moderately-sized rollover balances (e.g., $20,000 to $70,000) occur every year.[11] According to EBRI, in 2000, the average 401(k) balance was $49,000.[12] According to Fidelity's 2001 survey of 14,000 plans under its administration, the average defined contribution balance was even higher at $55,000.[13]

Like whitewater rapids, mid-life can mean rapid change, a rough ride, and unfamiliar territory. Consider the many issues your clients are facing: a mid-career job shift or a short retirement that leaves them so bored they are eager to start a new business or a second career. The kids may be returning home. Aging parents may need elder care. Those who had children later in life may still be grappling with college tuition bills. Second or blended families can double all the issues. Navigating the "whitewater" of mid-life, your clients will benefit from having a guide in their boat. A financial advisor who not only has expertise in financial products but also has some sense for this river of life, one who can provide a heads-up about what might be downstream, can play a vital role.

This is the role that you, as the Chief Retirement Officer, will play. As CRO, you become the experienced guide through the rapids. You have the tools and the expertise to help see your clients through the turbulence.

Chapter 4

HOW LAWMAKERS ARE PAYING YOU BACK

While the winds of change bluster and workplace and retirement issues swirl on whitewater currents through rocky rapids, there is a financial resource people can turn to and a tool that advisors can use to help them: Individual Retirement Accounts (IRAs).

Jeff's Rollover Success Story

Jeff left an executive position with an educational publisher after his company merged with a larger company. He had substantial assets—in the middle six-figures—in his company's 401(k) plan. As he considered his options, he started to seriously look at returning to teaching, his first love. While he did consider leaving his 401(k) in the company's plan, he wanted to feel he had more control over his investment options. He had always maxed out his 401(k) contributions, although he did have one small IRA account he'd started early in his career. He didn't add to it over the years because his income was always over the limit of being able to put money aside in a tax-deductible IRA. When he consulted his financial advisor during this transition, he learned about the tax-free growth possibilities of Roth IRAs. He also learned how he could take a more active role in overseeing his retirement investments by transferring his 401(k) account from the custodian directly into his formerly languishing IRA.

Building on the Potential of IRAs

Individual Retirement Accounts were created in 1974 when President Ford signed ERISA: the Employment Retirement Income Security Act. In 2001, the Economic Growth and Tax Relief and Reconciliation Act (EGTRRA) created many more changes. It's the most comprehensive tax act since The Tax Reform Act of 1986. This legislation has simplified some retirement account issues while opening up opportunities for workers, investors, and their advisors.

In a trend that has only accelerated over the past decades, legislators, in their own inimitable way, have encouraged taxpayers to take responsibility for saving for retirement. Increasing personal responsibility for retirement planning is now even more urgent.

The visible cracks in two legs of the three-legged stool of retirement, specifically the pension crisis discussed in Chapter One and the Social Security funding crises, pose a serious threat to the retirement plans of an entire generation. Since that generation is the Baby Boom, we know that whatever happens, this pig-in-the-python population bulge will make radical changes to the whole retirement scenario.

We moved from government providing for retirement to big companies providing for retirement. Now, the responsibility for the Baby Boom generation's retirement income will be their own.

For years, advisors were sometimes reluctant promoters of IRAs, with their hefty paperwork quotient and relatively small base of assets for any given individual. I want to argue, however, that those pain-in-the— — IRAs are now potential hidden jewels of opportunity for advisors.

Let's look at those millions of IRA accounts (and many of your clients and prospects have more than one IRA account!) as treasure chests of wealth for an entire generation. Better yet, consider them magnets, attracting assets from all over. You'll see why as we consider how this legislation is paying you (and your clients) back.

EGTRRA's Three Themes

The Economic Growth and Tax Relief Reconciliation Act of 2001, what I commonly refer to as "the legislative omelet known as EGTRRA," is a convenient starting point for our discussion. The legislation speeds up the trend of shifting the responsibility for providing retirement income to the individual. The EGTRRA legislation ran 417 pages. This hodgepodge of rule changes offered no grand themes, no sweeping declarations, no romance, no intrigue, and not even one chase scene. Some readers even say this doesn't seem to make any logical sense. Where is the motivation?

In general terms, there are three themes going forward in any legislation that will affect the ability of Americans to save for retirement. EGTRRA makes significant changes to all retirement plans in these three primary areas. First, workers can contribute more. Second, all plans are becoming similar. Third, there is increased flexibility to move from one kind of plan to another—portability.

Increasing Contributions

Workers can contribute more, and gosh darn it, they need to! If the Baby Boom generation doesn't start saving for retirement, then we are all in a heap of trouble. So, every single plan out there can now accept a higher level of contributions. Individuals older than age 50 can put in even more money.

Here are some of the key highlights of the ways participants can now contribute more:

- The disparity in annual contribution limits between governmental 457 plans and other qualified plans ended in 2002 when the maximum contribution increased from $8,500 to $11,000.

- Thereafter, all qualified plan contribution limits rise to $15,000 by 2006.

- Contribution limits to IRAs increase as well, rising from the current $2,000 to $5,000 in 2008.

- The law allows individuals age 50 or older to make additional, annual contributions (rising from $1,000 in 2002 to $5,000 in 2006) each year of participation in a plan. Additionally, current law allows contributions up to $15,000 for the three years preceding an employee's normal retirement age.

- This limit doubles to $30,000 by 2006. However, this catch-up provision must be used independently of the increased annual contributions available to individuals aged 50 and older.

- As a further supplement to increased contribution limits, beginning in 2003, EGTRRA allows 401(k), 457, and 403(b) plan sponsors to permit voluntary contributions to a traditional or Roth IRA operating in conjunction with the employer's plan—so-called "sidecar IRAs." Sidecar contributions do not count for purposes of the limits on contributions to the employee's 401(k), 403(b), or 457 plans.

Increasing Similarity

All plans are becoming similar. For corporate, nonprofit, education, municipal or government workers, as well as small business owners, all plans are looking the same. Whether enrolled in a 401(k), 403(b), or a 457, SAR, SEP, SIMPLE, eventually workers are going to have a 40___( ) — fill-in-the-blank, or some other acronym. Some of the key results from the EGTRRA legislation mean that all retirement plans will begin to look more alike.

These contribution increases recognize that over the past 20 years, Congress lowered the annual dollar limits on contributions workers could make and benefits they could accrue, in an effort to reduce the federal deficit.

As the percentage of the U.S. population over age 65 rises from 12.8 percent to more than 20 percent over the next 40 years and, more immediately, as the Baby Boom generation nears retirement, EGTRRA establishes mechanisms to help accelerate their savings.

By giving workers in the public and private sectors an equal chance to invest for retirement, not bound by such strict contribution or investment-type limitations, funding one's own retirement (or at least a large part of it) is as realistic for a teacher as it is for a doctor.

Portability

Now, workers can move their funds from plan to plan. The plans no longer have to be the same. EGTRRA allows virtually unlimited rollovers of pre-tax and after-tax dollars between 401(k), 401(a), 457(b), 403(b) plans, and IRAs. Expanded portability provisions encourage employees to take their plan assets with them when they separate from service, whether into another employer's qualified plan or into their own IRAs.

With the rapid changes in the employment sector (as discussed in Chapter Three, *Rethinking Work*), with increasing job changes, and with more downsized employees following a free-agent path, one of the most important factors in the EGTRRA legislation is pension portability.

EGTRRA liberalizes portability of retirement assets allowing workers to transfer their retirement savings from one job's plan to either another employer-sponsored plan or to an IRA. Past law restricted rollovers of pension assets in 401(k) and 403(b) plans to the same type of plan or an IRA. Past rules governing 457 plan assets restricted rollovers even more, limiting transfers only to other 457 plans. Effective January 1, 2002, EGTRRA allows rollovers to and from a 457, 401(k), 403(b) plan or an IRA.

Further, employees participating in state and local government retirement plans may use assets from a 403(b) or 457 plan to purchase service credits for prior years of employment.

Improved portability provides plan participants the opportunity to consolidate their retirement assets as they move between employment in the public, private, education, and nonprofit sectors.

Why IRAs Are Important to the Future of Retirement

All of these retirement funds can move to an IRA, which is a critical point for financial advisors. It's the biggest and best thing that legislation has done for financial advisors in a long time. Suddenly, that sleepy, underutilized IRA account is about to become the centerpiece of most people's retirement assets due to job-hopping, pre-retirement downsizing, rollover opportunities, and moving from corporate to nonprofit, education to business, and big companies to small.

These new portability rules are paving the way for the humble IRA account to become the depository of wealth for an entire generation. Whether clients have added contributions annually, or the distribution comes from a retirement plan at a former place of work, or it comes as an inherited IRA on the death of parents: all the money is flowing into an IRA.

You have to get your clients' IRA accounts. This is the vehicle that will allow financial advisors to provide advice on retirement investment assets as Americans' wealth moves to IRAs. As the money in IRAs grows to include rollovers from 401(k) and other plans, the decision-maker for all those IRA accounts is the individual.

You as the advisor must be prepared to initiate a conversation with clients and prospects about the most important investment account they have—their IRA. Why? Because 78 percent of IRA rollovers come from your own client base (See Figure 4.1).

EGTRRA Meets IRA

How will EGTRRA affect your clients' futures? How will it affect your future? *The future of retirement planning is affected because it now concerns one primary retirement vehicle—the IRA.*

Remember that EGTRRA allows 401(k), 457, and 403(b) plan sponsors to permit voluntary contributions to a traditional or Roth IRA operating in conjunction with the employer's plan—so-called "sidecar IRAs."

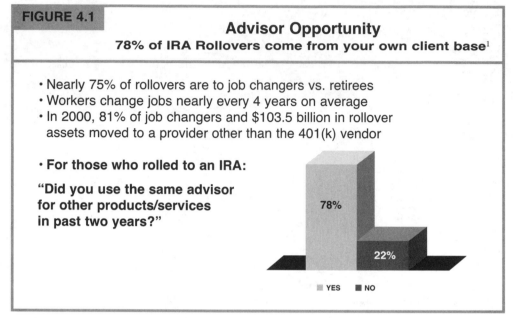

FIGURE 4.1

Advisor Opportunity
78% of IRA Rollovers come from your own client base[1]

- Nearly 75% of rollovers are to job changers vs. retirees
- Workers change jobs nearly every 4 years on average
- In 2000, 81% of job changers and $103.5 billion in rollover assets moved to a provider other than the 401(k) vendor

- **For those who rolled to an IRA:**

"Did you use the same advisor for other products/services in past two years?"

78%

22%

■ YES   ■ NO

Source: Spectrem Group

It also raised the limit on IRA contributions to $5,000 annually. It also made it possible to roll over your 401(k) to a 403(b) or a 403(b) to a 457—for those who have somewhere else to go.

For those who *don't* have somewhere else to go, there's only one place for those assets to go. Unless they remain in the previous employer's plan, they need to move into an *IRA*. These are people who have taken early retirement; or their jobs have been eliminated as part of a layoff; or they're planning on working part-time at a different job or in a different industry.

And let's not forget that many individuals believe that they—not the government or other sources—are responsible for their own retirement.

Here are three IRA Action Points for financial advisors:

1. For any current IRA account holders, make sure they know the increasing amounts they can contribute each year. Focus on the Roth IRA that has more generous income guidelines for being able to contribute the maximum (Remember with the Roth IRA: money goes in after tax and is tax-free coming out).

2. For clients over 50 years-old, emphasize the additional "catch-up" dollars

they can kick in to those retirement accounts each year.

3. Talk to clients about consolidating IRA accounts for better convenience and improved control.

The opportunity is large, as Cerulli Associates estimate that annual contributions to rollover IRAs will grow from $141 billion in 2001 to $402 billion in 2011.[2] The demographics will continue to make this a lucrative market. Asset growth has been tremendous. What will happen over the next decade is that the wealth of an entire generation will be given to the individual participants via their retirement accounts.

According to Employee Benefits Research Institute and Spectrem Research, job-changers and retirees typically own an average of three IRAs. Over a one-year period from mid-1999 to mid-2000, almost 10 million individuals either withdrew money from a qualified plan or had the option to do so. The balances involved in these decisions totaled $402.5 billion. These balances arose from all types of retirement plans, most often either a 401(k) plan (50 percent) or a defined benefit plan (23 percent).[3]

Distributions Options from Retirement Plans

The accumulated wealth of the Baby Boom generation will be heavily concentrated in employer-sponsored retirement plans and IRAs. The concept for these tax-deferred vehicles has been pretty simple up to this point: contribute the maximum to take full advantage of the plan. The value-added for the financial services industry has been on the asset allocation side of the business. As the Boomers approach retirement, their challenges will come in making wise distribution choices.

We will concentrate on lump sum distribution options from qualified retirement plans. A lump sum distribution from an employer's qualified retirement plan occurs when a distribution of the participant's vested account balance is made within one calendar year. Distributions can be made for several reasons: death, disability (except for self-employed), separation from service, (except for self-employed), and attainment of retirement age.

A plan participant has several options upon terminating from service:

1. *Stay with the Plan.* Provided the participant has an account balance greater than $5,000 (1999 limit), the plan generally cannot force him to leave unless the company is terminating the plan.

2. *Move It to the New Employer's Plan.* The new employer's plan must allow for rollovers. EGTRRA also allowed for more movement between different plans.

3. *Take a Cash Distribution.* The employer will be required to withhold 20 percent of the distribution and forward it to the IRS as a prepayment of income taxes owed on the distribution. The participant may not owe the IRS this much; the difference is refunded when she files taxes for that year. If under age 59 1/2, there is a ten percent penalty on the distribution amount, and current income tax is owed on the distribution amount. There are different ways to pay the tax as needed:

   • *Pay the taxes owed based on current income tax bracket.*

   • *Use ten-year averaging method.* For those born prior to 1936, taxes are paid in the year of distribution but the IRS treats the distribution as if it was received over a ten-year period. The 1986 tax brackets determine the tax liability. In order to use the ten-year forward averaging method, IRS Form 4972 would be attached to the individual tax return. A tax advisor can break this down further and explain the tax consequences of taking retirement plan money this way.

   • *Take a lump sum distribution and net unrealized appreciation* (no 20 percent withholding on the fair market value of the stock). Deliver the stock to the individual and pay income tax on cost basis, provided by the company. Pay long-term capital gains when stock is sold, provided stock was held for at least 12 months post-distribution.

4. *Create an Annuity Option.* An annuity is a "stream of payments" paid according to the terms of a contract. It begins at retirement age (65-years-old) and ends at the death of the participant and/or the beneficiaries. Distributions are taxed as current income when it is received. It is a guaranteed payment upon retirement. Generally, the account balance must exceed $5,000 (1999 limit). Payout will begin at retirement age (commonly age 65) as determined by the plan document.

An annuity is a contract issued by a life insurance company. It enables the participant to funnel assets into a number of different types of investments such as variable or fixed account vehicles, and it provides periodic income payments—either fixed or variable—down the road. A contract will be purchased from an insurance company.

Once purchased, all responsibility for paying becomes the obligation of that insurance company. The annuity contract will provide benefit options. Note, however, that if the participant is married when retirement benefits from the plan begin, the spouse must properly consent to the election of one of the alternative benefit options.

5. *Move to an IRA Account*. There are two options for tax-free movement to an IRA: a rollover or a direct transfer.

In a *rollover*, the employer will be required to withhold 20 percent of the distribution and forward it to the IRS as a prepayment of taxes owed on the distribution. The plan participant must roll over 100 percent of the distribution (which includes the amount withheld by the employer) within 60 days of receiving the distribution. If plan participants cannot come up with the money from another source, they will be taxed at the current income tax rate on the amount not rolled over, which is the 20 percent the employer held. If the participant is under age 59 1/2, an additional ten percent penalty applies on the amount not rolled over.

The *direct rollover* option would result in no withholding, no penalty, and no income tax paid. The money is moved directly from the account in the employer's plan into the IRA custodian.

Why Will They Choose You?

The distribution from a retirement plan represents one of the largest "money in motion moments" in the life of an investor. At a time of increasing change in their lives, and traditionally at an age investors should start to consider estate-planning procedures, this will be a moment for advice.

The Age of Advice is starting. An opinion issued by the Department of Labor (DOL) in December 2001 opens the way for plan providers to retain outside advisory firms to deliver a full spectrum of advisory services. The DOL stated that retirement plan providers no longer need special permission to offer participants consolidated investment management services—advice, asset allocation and portfolio management—as long as an independent provider delivers the services. [4]

Distributions from retirement plans go to the person who has the IRA account. As an advisor, what should worry you is that your clients have more than one IRA. You know they do because they call you and ask, "What's your IRA paying?" That means the other one is at the bank.

Do you know why that's important? Because that distribution from the IRA is a double-edged sword. You will either get it or you won't. No one will split the ticket. So you have to get that IRA. Realize that this is a non-negotiable point. Start thinking of the IRA as a magnet for your clients' future wealth because that's where the money from the downsized executive is headed.

Realize too that the issues of structural unemployment and the world of free-agent workers, combined with the demographic aging of the Baby Boomers and companies laying off older workers, mean that these distributions will come sooner rather than later. Within the next few years, your clients are going to get one of the largest checks they've ever been handed. Likely at the same time, they will be put in one of the most stressful situations of their lives: the loss of their life's work. What you have to decide is why they will bring that distribution to you rather than their other IRA vendor.

Legislation Pays Workers Back and Creates Opportunities for Advisors

This market is designed for one-on-one, face-to-face dialogue. The individual financial advisor has never been in a stronger position. Over the next five years, over a trillion dollars will come out of retirement plans. Most of it will head to an IRA. Nearly every client and prospect probably has an IRA. On average, people have more than one IRA.

If you can position yourself to capture even a modest amount of projected rollover dollars, your can grow your business. Depending on your ability to market, to influence participant behavior, and to build brand loyalty before and during the distribution event, the upside potential for new assets could be far greater.

As the Baby Boom Generation heads to the first transition in retirement, often encountering this pre-retirement age downsizing event, a whole new crop of issues will come up. The value-added of the financial services industry will be the ability to understand the needs of clients and to guide them through the maze of procedures necessary to access their retirement money.

In the next section, we will consider the issues your clients will be facing and the questions they'll be asking. In order to influence and build brand loyalty, let's take a look at the decision-making process your client base is going through. As a tour guide to the stressful decision-making process, you will be able to provide the resources to help clients make the best decisions for their particular situations.

WHAT YOU NEED TO KNOW TO BE A CRO

"Life is a river and we each make decisions about how to navigate it. The way the river flows is changing. The river of the past was generally calm, somewhat predictable, and moderately manageable. The river of the future is more turbulent, unusually unpredictable, and much less manageable. Our river is changing and our navigation should be changing. Life on the new river means we must learn, not only how to expect change and respond to it, but also how to imagine it and create it."[1]
     - H.B. Gellat, Author

In his book, Gellat uses the metaphor of a river to describe the condition of today's decision-making. In this section, we will consider the changes your clients are likely to be going through and how you can position yourself as a trusted guide to these changes on the turbulent river. Today, your clients are living through the twists, turns, and rocky whitewater that are the norm in workplaces across the country. They would welcome an experienced river guide on the raft with them.

What Will They Look for in a Guide?
Guides know the river, recognize the rapids, and have experience safely getting through even the roughest whitewater. Navigating many trips down the river under varying conditions helps these guides determine the best angle to approach especially challenging rapids and to locate dangerous rocks or whirlpools. To lead clients safely through the river journey, they must know what to do. Experienced guides develop plans, exercise appropriate caution, and select the right paths every step of the way. Such guides literally hold their clients' lives in their capable and experienced hands.

Likewise, as CRO, you will be handling most, if not all, of your clients' retirement funds. You will hold in your hands their future ability to "make it" to 59 1/2, 62, and 100 (We'll talk about what that means in Chapter 13.) To qualify as their guide, you bring care, skill, prudence, diligence, and an established process to address their long-term investing needs. You also have the tools of an experienced financial guide on hand.

As the winds of change bluster around the Baby Boom generation headed toward retirement, financial advisors can play a critical role as "whitewater tour guide" through the changing conditions. This second section focuses on the stresses and uncertainties your clients face and on how you as CRO need to proactively promote your role as their fiduciary in order to build their trust in your ability to help them with their finances.

It all starts with the stress that workers are facing. Some are doing a job that three people used to do. Some see their department's work being outsourced to cheaper labor markets around the globe. Some see their pensions disappearing or their costs for health care benefits increasing. Others are doing well. They know they have a limited window to maintain that income stream, and so they max out their work schedules to maximize out their variable pay—performance bonuses, commissions, or profit sharing.

Already under severe stress, some workers then experience the ultimate workplace loss. They are downsized. Their work is outsourced. The company goes into bankruptcy. They are offered the "early retirement" package. Their loss of livelihood often results in profound grief.

As CRO, you are a key advisor to your clients. The financial issues you are prepared to help them with may need to be put aside for a moment as you support them through the larger "life purpose" questions they may be grappling with during an event of such magnitude. Such a counseling role is not your main function. Yet for these times, understanding stressful decision-making, empathizing with your clients in their grief, being able to point them to the positives in the uncertainties they face, are some of the particulars that you will need to know to be a CRO.

Being let go from a work situation through downsizing or early retirement adds stress and a component of grief to the lives of your clients. Although you're not in the business of grief counseling, it's likely you will be called on to be a witness to the grief your clients are experiencing. You can help them address the many practical questions and changes, even as you acknowledge their emotional pain.

As their CRO and financial advisor, you can offer a human response, adding a powerful intangible to the already high value of your services. This will dramatically set you apart—in a category by yourself. What do you need to know? What will you need to do? We will address these questions in the context of the work-life-financial events your clients encounter.

Working through this section, you will learn how to handle your clients' concerns at each stage of their thrilling, albeit treacherous, journey through the work-life whitewater. You will track the timeline of their journey—from the moment they encounter the challenges of being right-sized through the stages of their stressful decision-making process. You'll learn the keys to help them take a positive approach to the uncertainties in the river ahead. You'll understand the key role you play as fiduciary, which is earning the trust of your clients.

Like the people on the raft trust their river guide, your clients must be able to trust you to be aware of the rapids ahead and to help them navigate the dangers. Like the fiduciary you are to your clients, you not only will *know* the right thing to do, you will *do* the right thing on behalf of your clients.

Chapter 5

STRESSFUL DECISION-MAKING

Ed and Janine Encounter Hurricane Andrew

Ed and Janine decided to cruise Bahamian waters in their yacht in the summer of 1992. "We thought we might run into some tropical storms, but we studied the weather patterns and storms over the last couple of years and thought we were safe." They discovered how easily it is to be fooled into a compromising situation. They learned what it feels like to have no place to run.

On August 19th, tropical storm Andrew was packing 50-knot winds and moving at 20 knots. By August 22nd, Andrew was upgraded to Hurricane, but "Bahamian radio was predicting the center of the storm would not pass within 30 miles of us." A hurricane in tropical waters is influenced by trade winds, and so it is difficult to make accurate predictions concerning the path. "I knew that Andrew was getting too close for comfort, but not close enough to know which way to run. I have never faced a decision that was so sharply attached to the difference between staying alive or not."

Ed continues, "We decided to go ashore at Chub Cay. At 5:00 am the next morning, reality started to sink in. Satellite pictures from the National Hurricane Center in Miami showed Andrew was headed straight for us!"

"By 11:00 am, the Bahamas Radio Network had pre-empted all programming and was broadcasting evacuation orders and shelter

locations. Chub Cay was deserted except for the two police officers and us. They had volunteered to stay and look after the situation. The strongest building on the island was the chapel, and we used it as a shelter."

"By 1:00 pm, Andrew was blowing maximum sustained winds of 150 MPH. There was a noticeable drop in temperature. A steady roar of unbelievable forces wrapped around us. Our ears hurt and popped from the pressure beginning to rise as the hurricane swept directly over us. At first, it was hard to breathe from the amount of wind. Seawater in the form of a fine mist blew in horizontal lines. Visibility was nil and our eyes were aching from the pressurized saltwater spray. Loud cracking noises were emanating from the roof. Everything was vibrating. The whole storm went by in 30 minutes."

"When we stepped outside, it was a different world. Hundred-foot-tall trees, with roots 30-feet in diameter, were lying all around. I could not find the stone gates leading to the marina. Chunks of hotel roofs, broken furniture, and pieces of buildings lay intertwined with mature trees. Out of all the buildings on the Island, only our little chapel survived. Based on the destruction, we all agreed that the building would not have lasted much longer. We were all very happy to be alive."

Hurricane Andrew left a trail of destruction in its wake. Such storms also leave thousands of its victims with a damaged sense of balance. In addition to restoring buildings and replacing material possessions, victims may need to devote time to restoring their own emotional equilibrium. They experience loss and grief. The decisions people have to make in times of shock are examples of what I call the "stressful decision-making process." In the early stages, people feel "numb and dumb."

Hurricane Precautions

As a hurricane approaches there are many precautions that people can take to prepare their homes for severe weather. The most important advice is: *do not wait until the hurricane is approaching to decide who is going to be responsible for specific tasks. Have a plan and rehearse it.*

The Federal Emergency Management Agency and the American Red Cross have developed a "Family Disaster Plan." Their four steps to safety are:

1. Find out what could happen to you.
.2. Create a disaster plan.
3. Complete their safety checklist.
4. Practice and maintain your plan.[1]

Then, if disaster strikes, remain calm and put your plan into action.

The Workplace Hurricane

I'm here to tell you there's a workplace hurricane on the horizon. This is arguably one of the most important stories you need to know to be a CRO. The planning you do with your clients is the equivalent of the "Family Disaster Plan" and its four steps to safety are listed above. To get your clients to develop a plan, you have to tell them the story and get them to take action before the storm hits.

Not everyone will have a plan in place when they come to you. Clients who lose a job, whether through downsizing, mergers, early retirement, or outsourcing, are very likely to go through the several stages common in the grieving and loss process. Just like the millions who live through the destruction of hurricanes, your clients experiencing the workplace hurricane can go numb after disaster strikes. The process of making decisions in that stage is filled with stress. Often accompanying the grief is stress related to financial matters. Consider this: these are people who, often in mid-career, are forced to rethink their lives and livelihood, and at a moment when their finances may not seem to offer the luxury of extended consideration.

We're talking here about the specifics you need to know to be a CRO, not a grief counselor. However, if you want to be a Chief Retirement Officer to clients encountering these stages of grief and the stresses that result from the loss of their livelihoods (and potentially that's just about everyone), it is important that you understand the whole process: grief, loss, and the challenges clients will face as they try to make decisions from this stressful situation. See Figure 5.1 for the top stressors your clients may be experiencing.

You will also be called upon to empathize with your clients as they work their way through the emotional stages. They will get to the point of being able to make financial decisions only by going through the grieving process and coming out on the other side. Like the river guide whose experience prevents the boat from flipping over through the rapids, your presence and experience can see your clients through each "whitewater" event in their lives.

FIGURE 5.1	What Are Clients Going Through?

The Top Ten Stressors[2]

1. The loss of a loved one
2. Major illness or injury
3. Divorce or separation
4. Serious financial difficulties
5. Loss of a job
6. Marriage
7. Relocation
8. A serious falling out with a close friend
9. Birth of child
10. Retirement

As ranked by the American Institute of Stress

Some clients will be suddenly more well off than they ever thought possible. Even in this situation, there can still be grieving issues in spite of hefty payouts. The daily work that has defined "who this person is," often for 25 or more years, suddenly *is* no more. They grieve for the loss of this identity, which is often closely tied to the workplace or position. Granted, you're a financial advisor, not a therapist; still, there are some "rules of the river" that you, as their guide through the rapids, need to be familiar with.

Advisors are coming into the industry by way of downsizing and rightsizing elsewhere. In my presentations, up to one-third of the attending advisors are living this trend of "bridge jobs," the second job or career after an early retirement or downsizing. These advisors can make an immediate and intuitive connection with clients and prospects facing an unexpected "early retirement" and all the life issues that go along with it. If you've been through similar experiences, *do not underestimate* the value you bring to the process!

For those who haven't been through the experience personally, it's still possible to understand clients in this situation and respond appropriately. I have experienced these unexpected career transitions and the resulting emotional roller coaster. I've also researched the grieving process to create a simplified approach for financial advisors to be able to truly serve the needs of clients going through this process.

Whether it's losing a job or a wallet, a spouse, child, parent, pet, or home, the magnitude of losses may differ, but the grieving process remains remarkably similar. Whenever there is change, there is loss—and loss always brings about some degree of grief.

At mid-life, when job loss often occurs, people are frequently experiencing other losses and changes as well. Loss on a more dramatic scale can result in post-traumatic stress disorder (PTSD), and this too requires people to go through a process for recovery. Wars, bombings, or natural disasters can fall into this category. While there may be some highly abusive or toxic work situations, PTSD-level trauma is generally not the norm in most workplaces. Still, the world is changing rapidly and in dramatic ways. Stress and loss go hand-in-hand. Multiple losses in a short span of time can profoundly affect your clients. Stress combined with multiple losses can increase the time it takes to work through the grieving process.

In order to become a tour guide to the decision-making process, advisors need to understand the process. Transitions in retirement, including early retirement, provide tremendous amounts of stress for the decision-maker. It's important to look at the role of stress and loss in the grieving process, and how it affects decision-making.

Stress

In the book *Future Shock*, Alvin Toffler observed that people experience more stress whenever they are subjected to a lot of change in a short time.[3] If anything characterizes our lives these days, it is an excess of change. We have less control and live with more uncertainty. For many clients, jobs and careers are the biggest source of stress in their lives, and that stress is simply increasing with mergers, downsizing, outsourcing, and early retirement. The resulting insecurities, uncertainty, and fear increase stress—defined as the inability to cope effectively with a threatening situation.

A threat to our livelihood can be especially stressful because so many people do not maintain adequate reserves, neither of time nor financial resources. Most are outspending their income through the "miracle" of credit cards. Many are only a paycheck or two away from financial disaster. And they are so busy and over-committed that they've left no time to consider their options.

Robert A. Karasak, Ph.D. and his colleagues at the University of Southern California have identified what they consider the recipe for a stressful job:

1. Find someone with a typical job.

2. Add lots of pressure to perform.

3. Add a lack of control over the work process, which equals a stressed-out person.

4. Now, add a changing organizational structure, which equals an extremely stressed-out person.[4]

> *"According to the New York Times, the University of California at Los Angeles has introduced 49 undergraduate seminars that focus on the psychological effects of living in our truly traumatic times...the angst that underlies the seminars sounds very familiar. It reminds me of the suffering people go through...when they are serving time in a job hunt."[5]*
>
> *— Carol Kleiman, Tribune syndicated columnist*

Working people are often stressed at their workplaces, either making up for work previously done by downsized colleagues, working frantically to meet goals and budgets, trying to balance important commitments both at work and home, or anticipating job loss. Today, it's likely to be all of the above.

Herb's Story—Out of the Blue

"It seemed like it came out of the blue," reported Herb. He was the leading sales associate at a high-end electronics store that prided itself on high-level customer service. He had won multiple awards and was among the top producing salespeople in the organization. Suddenly his skills were no longer needed. Management decided to change the focus of their sales force, providing vastly less customer service. With this new approach, the skills of someone like Herb were no longer needed, and more importantly, neither were his substantial salary and commissions. Herb had a retirement account with an advisor as well as one at his workplace. He visited his advisor immediately after losing his job. Herb was ranting, nearly breathless with anger. He was so angry that he didn't want anything to do with his old company anymore. His advisor asked if he had a 401(k) retirement plan with his former employer. Thinking about it, Herb realized he wanted his funds out of there—fast. Fortunately, Herb's advisor clued him in to a process that would save him money and aggravation. If Herb took possession of the money— even to roll it over into his IRA—he would get hit with taxes and penalties. By having his advisor do the paperwork to roll it over directly from the workplace retirement account to his personal IRA, Herb avoided the

penalties and tax implications. "Just get it into my own account," he said. "I'm too angry to decide about anything more than that right now." For the time being, he moved the funds into a money market fund, so he could make a more informed decision late—when he was ready.

In this case, the advisor had a client willing to make one decision (out of his anger), but he wasn't yet ready to make further decisions about how to invest the money. At least the advisor was able to provide assistance so Herb didn't make a hotheaded move to "get his money out of there" at any cost.

Loss and the Grieving Process

When people encounter loss, they go through a process of grieving. While grief experts offer variations on this theme, the stages of grief generally include shock, anger, denial, shame, and grief—all eventually leading to acceptance. Grief is a set of reactions to loss or the threat of loss. Financial advisors should know the predictable phases of the grieving process. Anticipating the stages your clients will go through will allow you to proactively support them through their grief and into healing. Ultimately, this can result in stronger relationships and more powerfully position you as CRO.

Noted psychologists, doctors, and authors have identified stages for the process of loss, grief, and acceptance of change. There are common themes running through all the works: reacting to the loss, reassessing the situation to come to terms, and finally, realigning in order to move on. Most people experience the stages as fluid, finding themselves in more than one stage at a time, or moving back and forth as phases overlap. A person's history of making and breaking bonds and reacting to loss will shape the way he or she deals with loss in the present. For those who want to explore these issues in more depth, we have included references in the Notes section.[6]

Grief includes feelings, attitudes, and behaviors that unfold over time. People react differently in terms of the degree, scope, and time it takes to go through the process. Failing to deal with grief leads to stress, energy drain, and negative attitudes. While grief is usually associated with death and the loss of loved ones, it can come from many sources other than death and dying.

The loss of a job can produce significant levels of anxiety and stress because work provides a sense of identity and a sense of purpose. People often define their social persona through their occupations. Work also offers relationships outside the family and gives people a place to develop skills and creativity. The traumatic changes taking place in the workplace have been like deaths to millions of employees and their families. However, businesses and society as a whole, have given short shrift to workplace grief. Their grief is real and normal—and there are ways you can help your clients through the grieving process.

Connecting the Grieving Process with Decision-Making

I've outlined a simplified version of the grieving process to help advisors recognize when clients are ready to make financial decisions. Initially, there's the *reaction*—they're "numb and dumb." Next comes *reassessment*, where they gather information. Finally, they reach *realignment*, where they experience the ability to make decisions and move on. Clients might come to you for advice at any point in the process, but most likely will approach you when they begin to gather information to make the necessary financial decisions. In Chapters 10 and 14, we'll also discuss the connections you, as CRO, need to make in order to proactively prospect for clients who might be in these stages of loss.

Step 1: Reaction to Loss

At this time, your clients are "numb and dumb" (survival instincts from their earliest memories), which manifests as a time of anxiety (anger, fear, despair, confusion, and helplessness) and wishful thinking (denial, regret, and bargaining). There is a yearning for a return of the lost situation or person, despite the impossibility of recovering what was lost.

Just like Herb in the story above, anger is a common reaction. People express anger either directly or indirectly. Feeling angry is not bad or wrong; but what is done out of anger can be bad or wrong. Direct anger is a hostile attitude, including words or behaviors. Grumbling, excessive questioning, complaining, arguing, committing acts of physical violence (and in some cases, homicide), have all been reported in the workplace. Indirect anger may be seen as decreased cooperation, lack of effort, and diminished self-direction. There may be resentment at having to prove oneself all over again, to redefine self, and figure out what to do next. There's irritation at routine disrupted. Workplace loss can bring about the dumping of anger on the old management, the new management, co-workers, or family.

For some people, denial is natural. Avoiding reality makes it possible for them to gather needed inner resources to adjust or develop skills. They don't want to let go of what has been so much a part of who they are. To let go of this piece of identity is allowing that part to die, which is painful. People seek to delay such pain, push it away, and pretend it isn't happening. Someone who is suddenly unemployed might aimlessly drift—doing nothing in particular for weeks, avoiding the problem as much as possible. Or they might do just the opposite and become actively involved in anything but job hunting, even evading discussions about it.

Avoiding the reality of the loss can also take the form of ignoring the significance of the loss, as evidenced in comments like, "No problem. I wasn't so crazy about the old job anyway." People can drift in and out of believing that change has taken place or is about to take place. Disbelief or inability to comprehend the loss is another manifestation of someone trying to avoid the harsh realities. These reactions occur most frequently during the early shock phase of unemployment. Inactivity and avoidance reflect automatic processes that protect beings from acute levels of anxiety by blocking tension build-up.

Despair, a period characterized by apathy and sadness, sets in as hope fades for recovery of the loss. The actual loss of people, work routines, location, identity, and self-esteem—along with the breaking down of old bonds, pulling away, and mourning—all can depress a person and reduce an individual's energy level. People may find themselves feeling out of control, helpless, and/or inadequate. The loss of stability and the need to continually adjust and readjust can create a feeling of a permanent "whitewater" phenomenon, or "When is it going to stop already?" atmosphere. As a guide to the "river," you may be able to validate their feelings as just a natural part of the process.

The pain of grief can be physical as well as emotional. Often a person who has experienced loss will say, "I feel like I've been punched in the stomach." Any type of loss can bring about those hurting, aching, and empty feelings. It is important that people allow themselves to feel these feelings and to tell someone about them as well. As a CRO, you might find yourself in that position.

Step 2: Reassessment of Loss Encompasses Information Gathering

As people traverse these various paths of grief early in the process, they begin to approach a point of acceptance. They go through the beginning stages of detachment and begin the reassessment process. An individual faces the facts that one stage is ending; that what was *is* no more; and that things will change.

Herb's Story Continued

So how did Herb deal with his loss a bit later in the process? His advisor called him to check in about once a month but didn't speak to Herb in person until the third monthly call. Herb reported that he had been out looking for work. They set up an appointment. Herb came in after one of his interviews, seemingly calm and assured. As he spoke with his advisor, though, Herb showed a few cracks in his well-polished facade. "I've been interviewing, networking, sending out resumes—all the usual stuff. Today was the first interview I've had for a position that even comes close to my previous job. It's still sales, but even with the commissions, it pays less than what I was making when they let me go."

Herb was quiet for a few minutes and then, with a voice shaking in pain, said he didn't know how he was going to make ends meet. He didn't break down in that meeting—not quite—but it was a close call. Herb knew he needed to make some decisions. By the end of the appointment, he was ready to listen to the suggestions his advisor was making and to learn how long his money would last without drawing on retirement funds.

Acceptance is primarily an intellectual state. The beginning of a new phase starts with the gathering of information and adjusting to the new reality. This is the stage that might encompass the search for a headhunter, career counselor, or coach. It's also the time when clients are ready to find out what their financial picture has in store for them. The successful advisor now gets clients to start thinking about the make-up of a portfolio and pulls out tools like financial calculators to help people see how long the money will last and how soon (or if) they will need to dip into retirement accounts.

Anger, hurt, fear, confusion, guilt, and shame are typical parts of the grief reaction. While clients may go through the majority of these reactions early in the process, they can slip into some of these earlier emotions even while in the information-gathering stage. It's important for advisors to be prepared for the human and emotional reactions that may resurface as clients begin to deal with important issues. The reaction is a psychological trauma just as a wound is a physical trauma. The grief process is an attempt to reestablish the individual's emotional balance in the same way that physical healing reestablishes the body's well-being.

Step 3: Realignment, Decision-Making, and Moving On

Realignment can only take place after completely detaching from the loss. Once individuals address their grief, they can begin forming new attachments. By facing the fact of the ending of what was and the notion that life will never be the same, they can begin to move into acceptance—a calmer, more regular part of their emotional landscape. It means they have accepted the inevitable. There is no exact timetable for the length of this process. Decision-making is possible only as clients approach this moving-on stage. It is the point where money comes into motion. Clients can make distribution decisions in a more clear-headed fashion.

If there's stress, and a decision can be made that negates having to make a decision, count on it—that's the decision that will be made at earlier stages in this process. Your clients will make the decision not to make the decision at all.

Herb's Story Concludes

Six months later, Herb was a new man. He'd learned from his advisor at the three-month point that he'd need about $10,000 in income for every month he was out of work. In looking at his non-retirement funds, he and his advisor worked out a plan. There wasn't much margin for error because Herb didn't want to get hit with more taxes and penalties if he drew on his retirement funds before he was eligible. Herb successfully cut back on expenses to the bare minimum and sold his sailboat to add to his cash position. At the end of six months, Herb was again employed. "Yes, it pays less than the old job, but it's only a few minutes from my house. Until I got this new job, I didn't realize how stressed out I got over that long commute. With all this extra time, I'm working on a sales consulting business. I know sales. Maybe I could help salespeople or companies increase their revenues—and earn some extra income for myself on top of it."

Herb is also putting away some of the money from his current position in an emergency fund—just in case there's a "next time."

How CROs Can Serve Clients Experiencing Stress and Grief

Attitudes and comfort level with people expressing their feelings can have a dramatic impact on whether staying with clients through this process is even possible for some. No one wants to deal with grief and pain. Most people want to avoid others who have experienced a tragic loss. There are people who see tears as a sign of weakness; anger as a lack of control; or worry as a lack of courage.

While our natural reaction is to push dramatic loss from our minds and to avoid people who are experiencing the pain of misfortune, the CRO can be most helpful when viewing the sounds of grief as healing. While you can't fix grief, your mindful presence and active listening can help a person who is going through the grieving process.

Each individual client will experience the pain of grieving differently. As CRO, it is important to be aware of the range of emotions that are possible for your clients who are under stress and grieving for their losses. What follows are some positive approaches you can use for yourself and your clients to usher them through the uncertainty.

Chapter 6

POSITIVE APPROACHES TO UNCERTAINTY

"I am an optimist—it doesn't seem to do much good being anything else."[1]
   - Winston Churchill

"I've never met a rich pessimist."[2]
   - Fortune 500 CEO

As a CRO, wouldn't it be nice to help your clients anticipate problems, instead of coming in after the fact? One of the most valuable services you can provide to clients is to introduce them to the story outlined in the first section, *The Winds of Change*. One of my goals is to prepare advisors to get out ahead of their clients, to understand what's happening in the workplace, and then initiate conversations *before* downsizing or early retirement occurs.

Ahead of the Curve

Any client who is between about 45-55 years old should expect some kind of downsizing or early retirement event. This is far sooner than most people are ready to retire. By explaining the story of *The Winds of Change* to clients, and then asking what they would do if it happened to them, you are going a long way to jumpstart their thinking processes. Some may actually take preparatory action in advance. That's an ideal to strive for!

In a sense, as an advisor, you may be introducing a topic that is not even on your clients' radar, but should be. Even with all the stories in the media, many people assume it will happen to someone else. By initiating this conversation with your existing clients, you are planting a seed. Then if the unthinkable does happen, you have already warned your clients.

In their anger, stress, loss, and grief, they will feel they have someone to turn to—someone who understands and who is competent to provide some answers. During the stressful time and grieving process, they will remember that you "predicted" this might happen to them. Who are they most likely to call when they are ready to start gathering information about their financial lives? Who will they turn to when they are at a point of being able to make decisions again? Who will stand the best chance of getting their rollover?

When they do come to you (at whatever point they are in the grieving process), the key is to listen, listen, and listen some more. Much of the help we can offer early in the grieving process requires active listening. You don't want clients to perceive as listening in a passive, disinterested way. If your attitude says to your clients, "When will this be over?" they will get the idea that you really would prefer not to listen. If you fail to make eye contact, let yourself be distracted by another activity, or change the subject, your clients will be aware of your lack of interest. You may discover that they end the conversation, avoid future discussions, and possibly cease to maintain or even terminate the investment relationship. See Figure 6.1 for client fears and ways to overcome their apprehension.

FIGURE 6.1	Karasik's "Four Fears"[3]

In a column titled "The Four Fears," columnist Paul Karasik addresses what a CRO can do to "understand how a prospect thinks and what prevents him from making the right decisions." Here are Karasik's four common investor fears—and potential solutions that the advisor can bring to the table:

1. For the fear of making the wrong decision, advisors need to assume the role of an educator, explaining why a particular investment was selected.

2. For the fear of change, advisors need to offer a road map for the process, so they know what to expect.

3. For the fear of giving up control, advisors need to continually ask for permission and agreement.

4. For the fear of losing self-esteem, advisors must communicate respect and concern and at the same time "always do the right thing. Always sell the right product to the right person at the right time."

Source: Paul Karasik, On Wall Street, August 2003

To be most helpful, listening should be active, allowing your clients to feel heard. To be successful as an active listener, avoid giving premature advice—and certainly don't try to "fix" their grief. Keep your attention focused on the other person, deferring to his or her agenda.

Sudden Retirement Grief

As you are actively listening to your clients, perhaps when there's an emotional flare-up during an information-gathering session, hold off on offering advice until they can focus on relevant issues. It's certainly not the time for talking about your own worries or making judgmental statements. It is still the speaker's agenda—and that should be respected. Questions, too, can sometimes stop a person's expression of feelings. We don't want to minimize the importance of letting your client vent these feelings.

Everyone goes through the grieving process a little differently—the timetable for mourning varies by individual. There is no right or wrong in this process. Your clients are just experiencing a normal human reaction to loss. It isn't easy to attend mindfully to another person's pain. Sometimes just listening and being truly present as they vent their emotions can be a tremendous help for people to process a difficult situation.

If clients are maintaining conversations with you as their trusted financial advisor and CRO, even as they process their grief over loss of work and livelihood, then as they begin to collect information in preparation for decision-making, you are exactly where you ought to be. In fact, as planner Olivia Mellan indicates, such listening is the first key to building the trust required to fully step into the role of CRO. In the May 2002 issue of *Investment Advisor*, planner Olivia Mellan suggests, "Helping your clients feel heard and then validated will build a strong bond of trust. Once your clients feel heard 'as they wish to be heard,' they will be much better disposed to take action with their portfolio." She continues, "In your body language, tone of voice, and facial expression, be careful not to communicate any desire to move along too quickly to closure and action. If you seem impatient, your clients will pick up on this and not feel safe enough to tell you all of what is going on. And until they do, they won't be ready to act on any of your recommendations, no matter how intelligent or appropriate."[4]

How You Can Help Your Clients Deal with Life's Uncertainties.

Radical changes are taking place in the workplace, our culture, the geopolitical situation, and virtually every realm that humans have to deal with. While the future has always been uncertain, the pace of change now pushes us to the limits of uncertainty. The rational, linear way of coping isn't always best.

As the river guide, you know that despite the placid water now, there are rapids coming just around the bend. How can you guide the boat—and your clients—safely through the rapids? A rigid "we've always done it this way" approach is likely to dump everyone into the river. Your experience, combined with the flexibility of having plans while knowing they are subject to change depending on the particulars of the situation, can be the attitude that guides the craft through the rapids. Your understanding of a flexible way of addressing life's uncertainties can greatly benefit your clients as they try to deal with change.

There will be times when your clients will be required to bring a sense of creativity, inconsistency, idealism, and instinct to their decision-making process. These traits do not fit with the traditional rational decision-making model. H.B. Gelatt's *Positive Uncertainty Approach* offers an interesting model of decision-making that is balanced and flexible. "Positive Uncertainty is a philosophical approach to making decisions about the future without knowing what it will be.[5] Here are the principles of the Positive Uncertainty Approach:

1. *Accept the past, present, and future as uncertain.* The past can be debated. The present exists as you perceive it. The future doesn't exist; it must be invented. "You must be the change you wish to see in the world," Mahatma Gandhi said. Gandhi's lesson is that change is an inside job. You get the change you want by identifying it and doing it. So, learn to plan and plan to learn. Set goals and devise strategies while expecting change to occur.

2. *Be positive about the uncertainty.* Reality is partly what you see and partly what you perceive it to be. Therefore, perception is reality—and you determine your perception. A good CRO will work at strengthening clients by first taking inventory of their strengths and then their perspectives toward "seizing the opportunity" that this job loss has created in their lives. You may want to share a story of another client who went through a similar trial and used it as an opportunity to segue into a career he had desired to explore.

Recognize that the principles of "knowledge is power" and "ignorance is bliss" can coincide. Many of the tools available to the CRO are great models for showing clients how to combine quantifiable information with a vision for the future. In essence, as CRO, you will be encouraging clients along these lines. "The more you know everything, the more you realize what you don't know." When you admit that you don't know, you open yourself—and an open mind is receptive to new learning and new use of your imagination. Creating your future requires that you dream—and then follow through on those dreams. Balance reality testing with wishful thinking. Practice envisioning desirable future scenarios as if they are self-fulfilling prophesies.

Making Preparations: Randi's Story

Even the financial world isn't immune to changes. Randi, a single mother and branch manager at a bank, had a good job and two children in school. It was a challenge juggling all the details of her job and children, but they were getting by. When another institution acquired her bank, it wasn't immediately apparent that there would be layoffs. Randi had been conscientiously putting aside ten percent of her income in the bank's 401(k) plan; but keeping up with that and necessities meant that she wasn't too many paychecks away from serious financial trouble—unless she dipped into that nest egg. In looking around her community as the merger proceeded, Randi realized that her branch might be vulnerable to being closed. She needed advice, and she didn't want to share her personal financial issues with advisors who were her bank colleagues. She found an independent financial advisor who recommended that she take out a home equity line-of-credit now, while she was still employed. By applying for this credit line now, and not using it, she will have an accessible financial cushion in case something happens to her job. It also means she will be spared going deeper into credit card debt or drawing down her retirement account in case of job loss.

"Playing defense: Before a layoff, take stock of finances and prepare— just in case"[6]

—Matthew Benjamin
US News & World Report

Randi is one of those fortunate, or prescient, people for whom the potential loss of a job isn't a blindsiding event. Or maybe she read the *US News & World Report* article. For many of your clients, the greatest service you can provide is introducing this conversation. It's highly likely that clients in the 45-55 age range will be offered "early retirement" somewhere along the way, and maybe more than once. While downsizing or mergers can happen to an employee at any age, as the stories from *The Winds of Change* indicate, the hardest hit will be those with the most years of experience—and hence, the highest legacy costs.

What Will I Do Now? What Will I Do Next?

Sometimes people are so close to a situation that they have trouble putting it in perspective. Financial advisor CROs can offer a valuable resource to clients, by helping them put the situation of loss into perspective. This broader perspective is another positive approach you can offer clients. Narratives such as the one outlined in *The Winds of Change* offer a more global context for the personal pain of a client's job loss.

When a client comes to you, either in the throes of the grieving process over loss of a job, or even the loss of a parent whose assets they will inherit, they are not usually prepared to make financial decisions right away. If a client is talking to her advisor about the loss of livelihood or the loss of a parent, the advisor who mentions that the portfolio needs a mid-cap mutual fund has just lost that client and her business. Why? Because you have not really "heard" the story your client was communicating. You've leaped past an important step, where the personal issues that needed to be dealt with weren't. And you lose.

Without a total commitment to *really* hearing clients as they talk their way through their grieving process, loss and stress, you will likely find that when they're ready to make that investment decision, they are working with another advisor. Those clients will move on to an advisor who will take the time to listen as they go through the process of grief. There's no specific timetable either. Patience is not only a virtue in this situation—it's a business necessity for a would-be Chief Retirement Officer.

> *"Age discrimination complaints filed with the Equal Employment Opportunity Commission have risen more than 24 percent ...The sharp increase, labor experts say, is largely attributable to the convergence of a weak economy and an aging work force—nearly 50 percent of the labor pool is made up of Baby Boomers, and the percentage of workers over 65 has increased from the last decade. There are now more older workers for employers to discriminate against, and more economic incentives to do so."[7]*
>
> *- Shaifala Puri, The New York Times*

When clients are forewarned about the story in *The Winds of Change*, when they are listened to as they go through their grief and stress, when they are presented with counter-intuitive tools for approaching uncertainty, then eventually they will be ready to make financial decisions—with you.

You will stand ready to assist them. This is where money comes into motion. They will be ready to make distribution and investment decisions. They will be stronger for having moved through their grieving process at their own pace. They will appreciate you for staying with them as they dealt with their loss. You have passed the first test of building the all-important bond of trust with your clients, a critical step to becoming a successful Chief Retirement Officer.

Chapter 7

CRO AS FIDUCIARY

"Communicating clearly is the essence of creating the impression of competence, skill, and mastery."[1]
– Harry Beckwith, Author

The Invisible Touch

In today's work-life "whitewater," consider what your clients see in the business news: corporate scandals, mutual fund irregularities, SEC investigations, etc. That's enough to make most ethical advisors cringe. How do you think your clients feel when they read the news about your industry and its highest profile practitioners? This kind of bad news on the business pages can affect the practice of a would-be CRO. How can an advisor avoid being tarred with that over-generalized brush? How can you communicate competence, skill, mastery, and trustworthiness? These are not nice add-ons. Rather, these traits are the keys for staying in business and staying out of trouble, which express the essence of your fiduciary duty.

Tom Olivo, founder and president of Success Profiles, Inc., conducted a two-year-long study of 1,500 financial services customers. Olivo asked them, "When it comes to working with your financial services professional, what trait is most important to you?" For those 41 and older, the number one response was trust and integrity. Its "relative importance" was 100 percent.[2]

Ethical Behavior in Challenging Times

Most advisors are good, ethical people. They act with integrity, look out for the clients' best interests, and treat their investments with professionalism. However, if there's not a solid relationship built on a foundation of trust and confidence, there's the strong possibility that even the best-intentioned advisor can be lumped in with that unsavory crowd. At the very least, given these business headlines, might your clients question the advisability of putting their entire retirement nest egg in *your* basket?

> *"Your Financial Advisor helps you with one of the more personal and sensitive aspects of your life–your personal financial security... First and foremost, this is a professional you trust implicitly. It's a trust of their competence, integrity, and objectivity, and a trust that this professional will act in your best interests."[3]*
>
> -AIC.dom

As you position yourself as CRO with the goal of helping clients with their entire retirement portfolio, what actions do you need to take to earn and maintain clients' trust with the resources they'll need to see them through the rest of their lives? What are your responsibilities and liabilities?

What is a Fiduciary?

According to *Black's Law Dictionary*, a fiduciary is first, "one who owes to another the duties of good faith, trust, confidence, and candor." Second, a fiduciary is "one who must exercise a high standard of care in managing another's money or property." A further definition of a fiduciary relationship is "a relationship in which one person is under a duty to act for the benefit of the other on matters within the scope of the relationship."[4]

A fiduciary's duty relating to retirement plans was defined in 1974, with the passage of Employee Retirement Income Securities Act (ERISA), and has been developed in practice ever since.

Here is a summary of fiduciary responsibilities:

1. Fiduciaries must run plan solely in interest of participants and beneficiaries.

2. Fiduciaries must run plan for exclusive purpose of providing benefits and paying plan expenses.

3. Fiduciaries must act prudently.

4. Fiduciaries must diversify plan investments to minimize risk of large losses.

5. Fiduciaries must follow terms of plan documents, as far as they are consistent with ERISA.

6. Fiduciaries must avoid conflict of interest.

Here is a summary of fiduciary liabilities:

1. Fiduciaries who don't follow these principles may be personally liable to restore plan losses.

2. Fiduciaries may be required to restore profits made through improper use of plan assets.

3. Courts may take appropriate action against fiduciaries who breach duties under ERISA, including removing them.[5]

Acting Like a Fiduciary

As CRO, the person whose goal it is to oversee your clients' retirement accounts, you must hold yourself to the highest ethical and professional standards. In fact, the client relationships you've been building—based on trust, integrity, caring, and skill—already approach the technical definition of a fiduciary.

> *"The concept of fiduciary duty applies to parties who deal with other parties' money."* [6]
>
> –*John and Ian Lohr, The Fiduciary Sale*

A fiduciary is not just someone who actively oversees other people's financial wherewithal, although that is the most commonly understood definition. If you offer investment advice, you may be held to the standards of fiduciary duty. These standards include doing what is in the best interest of the client and fulfilling your duties, as would a prudent expert. Fiduciary duty includes knowing your clients, making full disclosure of relevant information to them, proffering advice that is appropriate, and following an acknowledged and sound investment decision-making process that can be documented. Proactively explaining your process to your clients is an important step to helping them understand your recommendations.

Donald Moine in his *Morningstar.com* article, "Are You a Fiduciary?" points out that codes of conduct for CFPs, CFAs, and RIAs all indicate fiduciary responsibility. In addition, Moine adds that "the NASD holds that stockbrokers are fiduciaries."[7]

Some claim to offer education instead of advice as a way to sidestep the potential liabilities of fiduciary duty. While this may be a useful distinction for some, as CRO, you'll want to do both.

Execution of the fiduciary duty is not just a matter of picking good investment options or the right manager. The law requires that fiduciaries have a sound process in place to make decisions. For retirement plans, the Employee Retirement Income Securities Act (ERISA) requires the process be in writing as a formal "Investment Policy Statement." This is an ideal starting document for the CRO. In this case, the ERISA guidelines for fiduciaries overseeing retirement plans provide a powerful and commonly agreed upon benchmark for unimpeachable ethical behavior—exactly the highest and best practices that you, as CRO, will subscribe to.

> *"Whether a plan is subject to ERISA or not, the individuals determining which investments are available under the retirement program have fiduciary duties. For plans that are subject to ERISA, the fiduciary must act with 'care, skill, prudence, and diligence under the prevailing circumstances' that a reasonably prudent expert would use in the same circumstances. For plans that are not subject to ERISA...the standard is...based on the skill of a 'reasonable person.'"[8]*
>
> *- Kristi Cook, J.D., MCRS, NTSAA Legislative Advisor*

Financial Caretakers

When someone acts as a corporate or individual trustee of a retirement plan, that person becomes a fiduciary to the plan. This is a relationship imposed by law where someone has voluntarily agreed to act in the capacity of a "caretaker" of another's rights, assets, or well-being. The fiduciary owes an obligation to carry out responsibilities with the highest degree of good faith, honesty, integrity, loyalty, and service to the beneficiary's interest.

The "Prudent Man" rule is a fundamental principle for professional money management. As stated by the Supreme Court of Massachusetts in 1830, "those with responsibility to invest money for others should act with prudence, discretion, intelligence, and regard for the safety of capital as well as income."[9] It is a reference to what a prudent man would have done given the same set of circumstances.

To become the Chief Retirement Officer for your clients, you should look upon their assets as if you were a fiduciary to their retirement plan. I am not suggesting that you create a legal document, but at least formalize your process. The following plan encompasses the steps that a CRO should take to succeed.

What is the Significance of Being a Fiduciary?

The Department of Labor weighs in on the significance of prudence in being a fiduciary, saying, "The duty to act prudently is one of a fiduciary's central responsibilities under ERISA. It requires expertise in a variety of areas, such as investments. Lacking that expertise, a fiduciary will want to hire someone with the professional knowledge to carry out the investment and other functions. Prudence focuses on the process for making fiduciary decisions. Therefore, it is wise to document decisions and the basis for those decisions."[10]

What Does a CRO Do?

Developing an Investment Policy Statement (or in the case of the CRO's clients, a Retirement Policy Statement) can serve as a guide to the duties of a CRO. The minimum requirements for an Investment Policy Statement include the methods for selecting, monitoring, and evaluating investment managers.

A typical Investment Policy Statement includes the following subjects:

- Risk Tolerance
- Time Horizon
- Evaluation Methods
- Diversification
- Liquidity Requirement
- Rate-of-Return Objective
- Tax Considerations

This probably looks familiar; these are the "know your client rule" discussions. Because every investor presents a different situation, the CRO needs to gather all the relevant data to be able to put together an accurate Retirement Investment Policy. We'll discuss in more detail how to capture and organize all this information in the next section.

Once the investor and the advisor have established the Retirement Investment Policy for the client's retirement assets, the advisor must put the plan into action. Many plan trustees hire consultants to help with the investment, administrative, and/or legal aspects of running the plan. The consultant gives a plan trustee many benefits.

The typical processes that your plan consultants will conduct and document on you and your clients' behalf include:

- Investment Policy Planning (formalized in an investment policy statement)
- Asset Allocation Studies
- Manager Search and Selection
- Performance Measurement and Monitoring
- Trading Execution

As you can see, the assistance of a consultant to the retirement plan is quite valuable. Again, this probably looks like what you are already doing for your clients. That is because today's average high net worth prospect seems to have all the complications of a retirement or pension plan. These clients typically have two bank accounts; mortgage, personal, and equity lines-of-credit; 401(k), *contributory* IRA, *rollover* IRA, and direct relationship with two or more mutual fund companies; one full service and one discount brokerage account; a will; and an estate plan. More than likely, they hire an accountant for taxes and an attorney when dealing with wills, estates, or trusts (if they've gotten that far in their planning). These are important issues and are also intimately related to their retirement.

There should be a seamless plan that includes all these parts.

> *"As time goes on, we realize we don't really have enough time to try to learn everything; we simply have to surround ourselves with people we can trust to advise us."[11]*
>
> – Bill Bachrach, Investment Consulting News

With all the complexities, it is important that you take your CRO role to the next level, becoming "team leader" for these experts who work with your clients. Your goal is to help your clients marshal the needed resources and expertise. Your mission is to draw on those experts, while maintaining a focus on the entire retirement picture on your client's behalf.

If you want to act as a CRO, ask your client, "Do you know everything that you need to know about investing, asset allocation, distribution, and income and tax strategies, related to retirement savings, insurance, and estate planning? Do you want to invest the time and effort to learn about these issues?"

The fact is that most people lack the time to devote to these important aspects of their lives. We're busy. Many people are willing to pay for assistance, to find and work with someone with the specific knowledge, planning expertise, and disciplined process that can mean a more secure future.

Meet a CRO Who Takes a Fiduciary Approach

Tim Cooper enjoyed more than two decades of success in sales until a company downsizing in a troubled industry gave him the opportunity to look beyond what he'd always done. Tim, like many of your clients, made a visit to his financial advisor in the midst of his downsizing "event." Acknowledged as a top salesperson, Tim was unsure of his next move. He'd always enjoyed the annual visits with his advisor and took more than a passing interest in investing. One of the best things about his profession in sales was selling something he really believed in. Upon consideration, Tim decided to join the ranks of financial advisors. He brought his passion to providing a service he believed in to his new clients.

Well aware of the turbulence and confusion he had gone through during downsizing, and not really understanding his options or the future of his retirement, Tim made it his business to specialize in helping people who were going through exactly what he did. He considered how he would want to be treated and approached his new and developing client relationships totally focused on the long-term good of his clients. He took fiduciary responsibility seriously, creating "Retirement Investment Policies" based on his clients' needs. As trustee for his clients' plans, he took a leadership position, working with a consultant and other professionals who were helping his client—an attorney who works on wills and estates, an accountant, and even a banker. Tim also helps people who have to move, and so he has great contacts in relocation services.

Tim is especially excited about working with established entrepreneurs. Tim connects with people who not only need support in making sense of their own retirement plans but also want to put something in place for the benefit of their employees. One of Tim's conversations goes something like this: "What I do for my successful entrepreneur clients is customize and deliver solutions to their retirement plan needs. When would you have ten minutes for me to visit your office and learn more about your unique needs?"

CROs Stake the High Ground as Fiduciaries

To succeed as a CRO for your clients, you have to be willing to step into the role of fiduciary, acknowledging and affirming your responsibilities and commitment to clients. Some experts would argue that if you call yourself a financial advisor, you are in this position already, advising and overseeing their investment accounts.

A lot of what a CRO does are the steps that you are already taking with your clients—getting to know them and their needs, understanding risk tolerance, and allocating assets—all the basics that good advisors have mastered. Taking on the role of CRO simply reframes your opportunities to a higher level. While there are higher expectations, there are also greater opportunities to serve your clients while building your business.

You can—and should—build your fiduciary relationships with the everyday working people already in your book of business. While everyone else competes to serve the highest of the high net worth individuals, there's a huge and largely untapped opportunity to provide CRO services to those working people who have substantial or multiple IRAs or retirement plan rollovers—what I call "real people riches." The goldmine is already in your book. Building and affirming the bond of trust with your clients is the final critical step you need to master as CRO. Before we address the CRO's tools to encourage clients to take action, we will consider the importance of building trust in your client relationships.

Chapter 8

TRUST AND CLIENT RELATIONSHIPS

"Investor trust and confidence seem to be the holy grail of the securities industry. Precisely what investors are supposed to have trust and confidence in, though, has been somewhat fuzzy. Is it capitalism, the securities industry, the stock market, or the future in general? While big-picture concepts are important, the core of investor trust and confidence begins with the broker-client relationship."[1]

- On Wall Street

Sometimes there's an 800-pound purple gorilla in your office, sitting down with you and your clients. Always polite, neither you nor the clients mention this unusual guest silently in attendance at the discussion. This great unspoken? You are advising your clients on major life and financial decisions. They know, and you know, that you are getting paid for your services and/or the products you sell. They know you will be paid whether or not the recommended investments prosper. You are also in the position of having to "sell" your clients on taking the advice you have to give. You know, and you're not addressing these issues directly. Your clients know, and most of them aren't saying anything either. They're wondering, *"How can I trust that this is the right thing to do? Is this the right person to trust with my nest egg?"*

Like you, your clients read the newspaper and watch the business news channels. They've seen the reports about after-close trades in mutual funds. They've heard about bad apples in the financial industry, advisors who needlessly churn their clients' accounts to generate fees. Enron. WorldCom. These corporate scandals and industry misdeeds provided a wake-up call for working people everywhere. Maybe you know this isn't how you operate, but do your clients know? As CRO, you are a fiduciary who not only knows the right thing to do, but has a client process in place, and does the right thing by your clients each and every time.

Clients Natalie and Ray Ask, "Is There Anyone or Anything I Can Trust?"

"We're a little gun-shy," the couple admits. Two hard-working professionals, Natalie and Ray each had their own retirement funds with their companies but also had investments with a broker outside their company accounts, including a couple of IRAs. While their company accounts were invested in balanced funds, Natalie and Ray were planning to take a bit more risk with some of their non-retirement investment monies. "We took a big position in the technology sector at exactly the wrong moment. Our broker was gung-ho on high tech, even as the hot market showed early signs of cooling," notes Ray.

"When the market started going down, he didn't call. It seemed he was nowhere to be found," adds Natalie. "I know we are responsible, too, you know, for making the decision that we wanted to take on more risk with that money. But then he didn't even have the courtesy to call or even return our calls."

When Jack, a financial advisor, came upon Ray in an educational seminar he held at a headhunter's office, Ray was adamant. "I'm here to get information. That's all. I want to protect our family's investment accounts from our own mistakes as well as from the so-called professionals. I feel like we got burned badly by our last advisor who seemed more like a cheerleader for the high-tech sector than an objective advisor. One of the reasons I'm even in touch with this headhunter is that I need to find a job with a better salary to try and make up for some of the losses."

If you were in Jack's position, what would you do? How can one advisor build up a trusting relationship with a couple that feels betrayed? Trust between people is a powerful force. Its opposite, mistrust, is also a powerful force. Unfortunately, mistrust is rampant today. Mistrust is contagious and causes people to put up walls from fear, feeling they can't trust anyone. Mistrust is something that takes consistent and visible actions to overcome. Honesty, reliability, dependability, and consistency are some of the attributes that advisors have to exhibit as everyday behaviors in order to build their clients' trust.

Those news reports reaffirm a common question your clients are likely to have in these turbulent times: *"Is there anyone or anything I can trust?"* The relationships you are building with your clients should allow them to answer in the affirmative. "Yes. You know, my CRO is someone who really listens, understands, and offers good and relevant advice. I know most of these investments don't come with a guarantee, but together we've made the best decisions, given current information, that address my current and future needs. And we'll continue to review and discuss results because things are always changing."

Your fiduciary duty is a legalized version of trust. You're not selling hype. You're not the stereotypical used-car salesman. It's time to bring to the table a discussion about fiduciary duty, trust, honesty, and your client-centered CRO process.

Trust: The Basics of Connection

For those of you who take to heart the stories framed in the first section, you've introduced clients to the stories from *The Winds of Change*. You've helped your clients through stressful decision-making, even as they've processed their grief over life transitions, downsizing, and early retirement. You've given them tools to take a positive approach to the many uncertainties facing their lives and livelihoods. You approach your practice as a fiduciary. These are the building blocks that position you as Chief Retirement Officer.

Again and again I've learned from successful financial professionals that they never underestimate their task. "I've got someone's life savings in my hands," a financial advisor said to me. "And if I looked at it like it was a big ticket or a trade that will help me have a great month, then I just don't get it." Another advisor told me, "I have under my care 30 or more years of savings, the financial equivalent of each of my clients' whole lifetime of work. It's a responsibility I take very seriously."

What Is Trust?

Trust is the most important building block of your business. No matter how smart you are or how good you are at managing money, if clients do not trust you, you will never have the opportunity to become their Chief Retirement Officer. So, what is trust, and how long does it take to build?

In my dictionary, the definition of trust takes up six full inches, starting with trust in people, "assured reliance on the character, ability, strength, or truth of someone." One successful financial professional I know says, "Trust is established the moment a prospect chooses you over the competition. It is up to you to build or erode from that point." This sense of trust is something most people feel rather than know. You recognize that feeling—when you can depend on another person. What produces that gut reaction?

To be successful as a CRO, it is critical that your client relationships build to the point of generating that gut reaction—of clients trusting you. It is important because, as your clients go through the uncertainty and disruption of losing jobs and changing careers, they may get to the point of asking, "Is there anything I can really count on?" Your interactions with your clients should lead them to say, "Yes. You know what? I really can count on my CRO."

One of the consequences of the increasing speed of change is the loss of connection between people. John Naisbitt covered this point so well in his book *High Tech/High Touch*.[2] We are all wired for cable, linked to the Internet, but less connected to each other. No one, especially clients, will tell you they want to feel closer to you; it sounds strange. Yet, in an age of uncertainty, the foundation of success in all relationships is that feeling—it is trust.

To your clients, a connection matters more than the fee or return. Research shows clients regard their relationship with advisors as four times more important than investment performance in their overall satisfaction. Of the affluent clients who fired their investment representative, 87 percent did so because of relationship problems while 13 percent changed representatives because of investment performance.[3]

Trust Yourself

To maintain trust in our own professional futures, we as CROs need to have confidence in our abilities to make a difference to our clients. Simultaneously, we have to build our practices from the highest possible integrity and ethical standards. When we look to the troubles in the world, it's easy to throw up our hands and conclude we can't make a difference. I urge you to believe—and know—you can make a difference in your clients' lives by placing their well-being as your top priority.

Trust is based on honesty and respect and grows from sincerity and fidelity. You can depend on trustworthy people for truthful and sincere advice. It is my belief that your intentions are "to do what is right by the client." People who don't believe in doing what is right by their clients probably spend little, if any, time reading books that are based on a stated mission "to create long-term partnerships with clients and help them stay on track in meeting retirement goals." In addition, that dishonesty does little to help create long-term partnerships with people. I'll assume honesty or truth as a given. But what about reliability and sincerity?

Building Trust as CRO

Consistent behavior leads to the perception of dependability. Successful brands, services, and professionals are consistent. McDonald's is a good example. No matter where you go throughout the world, McDonald's is a brand that has built trust through consistent service and quality. People value reliability because it makes things more predictable.

What Might Jack Do to Build Natalie's and Ray's Trust?

Jack, our advisor from the story earlier, in his role as educator, has come across Natalie and Ray as prospects. There may be a possibility for Jack to earn their trust and turn them into clients. If he chooses, Jack can make a plan to consistently be in contact with Natalie and Ray, share relevant information, keep a conversation going, and make the case to them that not every advisor ignores clients. Jack can become a reliable source of information on the way to building a relationship.

Your clients should be clear about who you are and who you are not. They should understand your unique promise of value as CRO. This promise of value sets you apart from your competitors. It differentiates you and allows you to attract and build loyalty among the groups of people whom you can help achieve their goals.

Prepare a written statement of the services that prospects can expect from you. It might be a document called, "Duties and Responsibilities of a Chief Retirement Officer." Then go through the statement with them. As you cover each point, watch for their concerns and address them in detail. Be sure to ask prospects what they expect from you.

CROs should be able to articulate the process they go through with all of their clients. "*Here are the things I do. These are the things I require. This is what you can expect from me.*" Such reflects your clarity of purpose. In becoming a CRO, your actions speak louder than words. Your commitment to these principles will affect your day-to-day working relationships with clients.

The document should cover fees, commissions, or the costs of doing business with you upfront. "If there is a choice, outline the benefit of each, but offer the one that is fairest to that client," was the advice I got from another successful financial professional. He explained, "My success is a direct result of the referrals I've received from doing what is right by the client rather than the commissions I have received from the products I have sold them."

What about professional temptations? As fiduciary, you are putting those in the context of whether they fill the bill under the "Prudent Man's" rule. You also have at hand your list of working principles, "CRO's Duties and Responsibilities." But not everything is cut and dried. Let me give you an example. In general, IRAs don't need to be in annuities. That said, there might be specific client circumstances that strategically call for an annuity within an IRA. As CRO, your role is to explain the pros and cons of each side of the equation, and talk your clients through the reasoning behind your recommendations, which are based on helping achieve their goals.

Trusting Each Other

To gain the trust of or clients, you must combine the truth with empathetic listening. Asking open-ended questions and then *listening*, not only to the answers, but simultaneously "reading" the emotional state, attitude, and perceptions of your clients, is the key to expressing empathy. This ability to see others from their personal frame of reference and to communicate your understanding to the person involved, is the essence of empathy. To create supportive relationships with clients, you must be open and honest. On top of that, you have to be perceived as a good listener and a genuine person.

> *Remember this:*
> *To the client, a connection matters more than the fee or return.*

In addition, successful CROs demonstrate a caring attitude. Caring consists of understanding your clients' experiences and establishing a learning relationship with them. Ultimately, this sense of caring manifests in sharing yourself with another person in a way that makes a difference in both of your lives. With these attitudes in

> *"The affluent are concerned about whom to trust. In our survey, they said they place the most value on firms that uphold high ethical standards. That was more important than any other quality."[4]*
>
> *–David Irwin, On Wall Street*

place, clients will begin to open up with productive discussions focusing on their dreams, goals, and the financial challenges they need your help to address.

According to Todd Duncan in an interview in *On Wall Street*, "Brokers have to recognize that part of how they become the option of choice is by pursuing a path of differentiation, and the unconventional way of doing that is through trust. Many brokers have performance trust, which means that customers trust them from one transaction to the next…Relationship trust is deeper and more unusual. It requires intimacy and a broker frame-of-mind in which reputation and people are more important than revenue and profit. It requires brokers to use a disciplined, questioning process to find out what's important to the client concerning financial security and money."[5]

In the Wheelbarrow—and into the Future

There's a famous story featuring a tightrope walker crossing Niagara Falls in a gusty wind on the high wire. Nearly losing his footing in the wind, he was incredibly relieved to have made it across safely. Waiting for him on the other side was a fan with a wheelbarrow. "You're the best ever," raved the fan. "I believe you could walk back across pushing this wheelbarrow."

The tightrope walker shook his head and said, "No thanks," feeling he was lucky to have made it across once without a wheelbarrow.

The fan persisted, "I know you can do it. Just give it a try."

Finally, he said, "You really trust me, don't you?"

"Absolutely, I do," said the fan.

"OK, then," said the tight rope walker, "get into the wheelbarrow, and we'll start."

In today's uncertain times, I'd venture to say we're already IN the wheelbarrow—and on the tightrope. But, we do have a choice. We can choose to react with fear and denial and recriminations about who pushed us out here. Or, we can choose to trust each other and ourselves so that together we can get across safely into the future ahead. As CRO, earning the trust of your clients through great communication and living up to high ethical standards can lead to long-term success for both parties.

Building Trust as a CRO Opportunity

Trust in the future is especially challenging in these perilous times, with *The Winds of Change* blowing at hurricane speed. No one has a simple life or straightforward job any more. Further, as CROs, we are called on to project our confidence to the audience of clients. Our confidence grows out of trusting in ourselves and in our abilities to help clients. Those clients will gain not only trust in us and in the relationship with their CRO but also will increase their confidence as they learn the secrets of adapting to change and protecting themselves from catastrophic risks.

To achieve your own goals as CRO and to be successful means that you have to actively build trusting relationships. By doing so, you have an opportunity to make a good living as you help people make this difficult transition.

About that 800-pound purple gorilla…you must proactively address your clients' concerns, build their trust, and answer their question: *"Why should I trust you? You're getting paid to make these recommendations!"* Otherwise, that gorilla will only get bigger. It can be tamed by truthfully addressing the issues and potential dilemmas consistently and predictably. Having the conversation brings the scary monster to the table. It suddenly doesn't seem so huge and threatening. It becomes more like a purple, stuffed chimp.

Working together, like the tightrope walker and the fan in the wheelbarrow, together you and your client will build the needed agility to make it across the gulf—to deal with all that life presents. Such confidence is catchy! Building that confidence together with your clients will help you grow your book of business. What I call "real-people riches" acknowledges that the people in your book are the first people you need to serve as CRO. As you build relationships of trust, you're on firm footing to ask your clients to take action.

Even when your clients say that they believe an action is right, it may still be a difficult step to take. In today's world, things are changing so fast that we can hardly predict everyday events, much less the earth-shattering surprises from one year to the next. A natural reaction to uncertainty is to hold back. Yet, there's no security in standing still when the world is moving so fast. In the next section, we'll start by outlining what it will take to get your clients to take action so you can start to help them.

REAL PEOPLE RICHES:
THE CRO'S PERFECT BOOK OF BUSINESS

When the hurricane hits, everything changes. If you can find a way to present yourself and your work with clients as a port in this workplace storm, you will find weary and overworked prospects flocking to your door.

In my travels, I meet thousands of financial professionals each year. What I've discovered after 20+ years in the retirement end of the financial services industry is that the book of business of each advisor is a unique reflection of that individual. The "real people" in your book of business reflect, in some sense, who you are.

Right now, a lot of advisors and their firms are chasing "high net worth" individuals as clients. They are revamping systems so that smaller net worth clients aren't getting the personal service they once did. It's a mistake to think that only wealthy Americans should work with a financial planner. That's like saying only people who go on expensive vacations need a road map. Advice plays a critically important role in having a safe and secure retirement—no matter how much money is available. A CRO can help guide people down a path to making smarter decisions, indicating the array of choices to make *now* so they are able to live the retirement they are envisioning.

This approach is based on the needs of your clients. Whether they want to go mountain climbing in the Andes, volunteer at their local hospital, or spend more time with their grandchildren, your role as CRO is to help them develop the systematic approach to savings they will need to achieve their individual retirement dreams.

Based on what I've seen in the overall trends, there's an opportunity for advisors willing to start right where they are—with their current book of business. Growing your book by proactively soliciting IRA rollovers from current clients, their friends, neighbors, colleagues, and those in similar business niches, is the start of what I call "Real People Riches."

The hurricane story that's hitting workplaces, pensions, and retirement planning is coming on full force. It's affecting everyone—

real, ordinary everyday working people. The stressed-out, over-worked, potentially downsized individuals who are your clients now need your help more than ever. They are so busy that they are often willing to pay for services, as long as they perceive the value that's provided in return. Recognizing that these real people are well worth your attention is the first step to building a book of business that truly reflects your strengths—and your ability to address clients' needs.

Section Three addresses the myriad of ways that you, as CRO, add value. With the information in this section, we will explore how you can illustrate your value for those clients as well as for prospects who look very much like those in your book. Is this the right niche for you? I offer some questions for you to reflect on in Chapter 10, *Defining and Finding the Ideal Client*.

After considering all the changes that are rocking our work-places and traditional concepts of retirement, it's crucial to see this time of flux as presenting opportunities to better serve your existing clients, while attracting new clients, talking to likely prospects in your niche, and refining your practice-building model. We will continue to emphasize the importance of building your business via retirement accounts (currently IRAs)—the magnet for your clients' future wealth.

We will address how to get clients to take action, so that you really are in a position to help. What steps must they take for you to serve effectively as their CRO? We'll look at who are ideal clients for you, and how to attract more of them. We'll consider your role as CRO, and how you can present what you do in a way that shows the added value your clients will receive by working with you. You are a real person they know and trust. In an increasingly impersonal transactional marketplace, the personal touch makes certain relationships stand apart. There's a lot of value in that all by itself.

You will get a chance to reframe your tools to help clients address the lump-sum dilemma and provide suggestions for meeting their financial milestones:

- Making it to 59 1/2—when retirement funds can be accessed without penalty

- Making it to 62—when many can start collecting Social Security

- Making it to 100—acknowledging a dramatically expanded longevity that needs retirement funding

In this section, we will start to elaborate on the conversations you need to have at each of those stages. What are the issues your clients need to be aware of? How can you open the door to helping them achieve their life's biggest dreams and goals?

I will share some of the proven (but very simple) strategies for growing your business that are used by the industry's top producers. We'll look at what it takes to stay on top of your game as CRO. Maintaining what I call the "education edge" is key to your success and to continually improving your service to clients. Reading and analyzing the trends is both art and science. You will learn where and how I gather this information to access the big picture.

This section is full of action items, sample conversations, networking tools, and more that will enhance your value-added services. Here's a quick acronym, your G-U-I-D-E, to remind you of the action steps required of a Chief Retirement Officer:

Gather necessary information for decision-making.

Understand client's needs and retirement goals.

Invest retirement assets within pre-set parameters, helping build portfolios.

Develop reasonable expectations.

Establish benchmarks to monitor the progress of the plan.

If you are looking for ways to stand out in a crowded and increasingly undifferentiated or commodified field of financial professionals jockeying for business, you need look no farther. By refocusing what you already know and do, building on the current strengths of your book of business, and refining your practices to generate referrals, you will be positioning yourself as a trusted advisor, well-prepared to play a vital and responsible role in your clients' retirement planning—as their CRO.

Chapter 9

HOW TO GET CLIENTS TO TAKE ACTION

"The journey of a thousand miles begins with a step…"[1]
 - Lao Tzu

You've decided to build your business around your clients' retirement planning issues. Welcome to the ranks of CRO. Now what?

Ron and Samantha's Financial Check-up

Ron had two sons in college when he met Samantha. In the five years since his first wife's death, he had focused on his work and his kids. Now he'd delivered his youngest child to the ivy halls he'd call home for the next four years, except for occasional visits home on break and during the summer. Into Ron's almost empty nest came the engaging and energetic Samantha, called Sam.

Ron and Sam got married, and they immediately started a second family. By the time Ron's boys graduated from college, they had a couple of younger siblings.

Ron and Sam finally went to see Ron's financial advisor for a financial check-up, at Sam's urging. "I realized that Ron had taken care of college for his older boys, and I wanted our children to have the same advantages. Also, I know that Ron isn't getting any younger. I want him to have a good retirement. And frankly, I have some concerns about being able to help my own parents financially. I want to see if there's any way that we can accomplish all these financial goals."

Ron and his first wife had saved judiciously for their sons' college educations, sometimes to the detriment of their retirement accounts. They had married young, and Ron had a whole career in front of him. As he started his second family with Sam, Ron was much closer to the potential dangers of a midlife, downsizing event. When Ron and Sam visited with their financial advisor, and she talked to them about the workplace "hurricane" story, they knew there were some big issues they needed to face. When their advisor asked, "What would you do if Ron is downsized some time in the next five years?" They didn't have any answers, but they did have a lot to think about.

Your goal as a CRO is to introduce the workplace hurricane story and ask the "What would you do…" question to get clients like Ron and Sam to take action. That's what we're going to consider.

How the Coming Workplace Hurricane Spurs Action

Unless you can get your clients (and prospective clients) to take some action, nothing happens. You may have a nice title but won't get anywhere with your new mission. Let's start with where to focus your efforts, whether you're just starting out or looking to expand your business, in order to achieve the best results for you and your clients.

Many times, you meet prospects whose money is in a static position. They are happy with their current advisor and have no need to make a change. An easier and more powerful way to build a practice is to design your business around the times in clients' lives when money is in motion. Transitional periods offer unique opportunities because you are able to explain the resources you have to offer to prospects or clients. Distributions from retirement plans are an example of a time when money is in motion. You want to be positioned with the Rons and the Sams of the world for those times when concerns arise and when money kicks into motion.

Introduce the Winds of Change—Before Downsizing Hits

It is key to start this conversation with your clients before they are in the middle of the *stressful decision-making process* outlined earlier. Let's say their money isn't in motion—yet. Your 40- to 55-year-old clients are still happily employed, and maybe they are so busy in their work situation during their peak earning years that they neither need nor want to think about the future. On their treadmill of intense commitments to work and family, they can barely keep up with today! Often they are living from paycheck to paycheck, and debt is piling up. Maybe they're able to max out their 401(k)s. Or maybe not. Maybe they are planning for their children's college education. Many are so busy that they are willing to pay for services to help them cope.

You are ideally positioned to discuss the added value that your CRO services provide. The value-added conversation will be covered in-depth in Chapter 11, *Defining Your Role as CRO*. For now, the key is to help your clients buy in to having a CRO by getting them to take action so that you can more effectively help them both now and down the road.

You've learned that the work life of those 40+-year-olds is at risk, with down-sizing, offshoring, early retirement, and more. Even if everything is going well, there's still a one-in-four chance that they will change jobs and/or companies in any given year, opening the possibility for retirement plan assets to rollover to an IRA. As CRO, you realize that legislation has made workers completely responsible for their retirement. Most people don't understand the tough issues that will be coming at them. Many are ignorant of the weather forecast of a coming work-place/early retirement hurricane. In ignoring this, they risk outliving their financial resources.

I've always maintained the philosophy that we in the financial industry need to educate our clients first and make the sale after that. To that end, the most important conversation that will start to educate them is introducing clients to *The Winds of Change*. "If I told you that your company is going to downsize you sometime between the time you're 48 and 56, what would you do?" It is the possibility of catastrophe that will get them to sit up, take notice, and take action.

Prepare for Bad Weather

The process of putting on your "weatherman hat" and warning clients about the coming hurricane in their financial lives lays the groundwork for everything that follows. It's telling the story outlined in *The Winds of Change*. After the story of bankrupt pensions, layoffs, and more, you might then ask, "So, what is happening in your industry?" Or, "Is anything like this happening in your industry?"

Another way to start this conversation, after you've talked about *The Winds of Change*, is to ask clients, "What would you do if something like this happened to you? Are you prepared? How much emergency cash do you have on hand?" Or,

"What would you do if, at age 54, you are asked to redefine your life?"

If your client answers, "I don't know," then as CRO, you need to continue the conversation and begin to draw upon the many tools you have available, saying, "So, this is what we need to think about." Ultimately, that conversation is about how they want to live their lives, with financial models that indicate how long their money will last.

Introducing this story means helping your clients face potential catastrophe. The tools and resources you have available to help them are the building blocks for avoiding catastrophe—the life preserver for helping them weather the storm. It's easier to talk to your clients when they're not in the middle of the stress of downsizing. Now is the time for you to begin.

If they can exercise restraint and discipline, you might counsel homeowners to get that equity line of credit to have on hand as back-up—so they don't have to max out credit cards if they're laid off. By having the conversation before catastrophe strikes, it's more likely that when those clients are thrust into the time of stressful decision-making, you will be the financial professional they turn to. The IRA that you have will be the IRA that receives their company plan rollover. While they're still employed is the time to lay the groundwork of telling this story and to get copies of several key documents to ensure that you're the trusted advisor they turn to.

Get the Summary Plan Description (SPD)

"We'll keep a copy right here." Lawyers say that when a couple comes in to write or update their will. In the stress of a loved one's passing, attorneys realize how important it is to have access to the key paperwork they need to do their jobs. Nor is the bereaved going to read the will at that point. They will go to the professional who has a copy on hand.

In the catastrophe and stress of job loss, it's unlikely your clients will realize how important it is that their summary plan description (SPD) is accessible. Chances are, they don't even know what it is. Getting this document allows you to help clients identify opportunities and potential pitfalls associated with their employer-sponsored retirement plan. Every one of your clients who is covered by a retirement plan gets a summary plan description (which they most likely have never read). If you are covered by a retirement plan, you received a summary plan description. What are the chances that *you* have ever read it?

Apparently, I am one of the few people out here reading summary plan descriptions. They are written by young lawyers, and the pages are full of love, romance, and intrigue. No? A summary plan description will tell you about all the rules of a retirement plan.

Ask your clients about their summary plan descriptions (SPD). Your clients probably won't know what a SPD is—even though many had to sign a form with the Human Resources department to say they received a copy. You may want to use the "StorySelling" approach here, from the book, *StorySelling for Financial Advisors* by Scott West and Mitch Anthony. With StorySelling, you make the unknown known through the use of the familiar.

Here's one approach. "I need your summary plan description. It is the document that tells me all the rules for your retirement plan. It's like one of those 'Call before you dig' advisory posters. Think of your SPD as though you are digging in your back yard. You first need to call the gas company because if you hit the wrong pipe, you will blow up your house. The SPD will tell us where all those pipes or danger spots are for the most important assets you have."

Or you might try this. "You know how the pirates always went out to look for buried treasure, and they always had a map? That map is your summary plan description. It will tell us where all your retirement plan treasures are and how to get to them."

Why do you want the summary plan description? When your clients are let go by their corporations, two people will have their summary plan description: you and the Human Resource people that hired security to take them out of the building. And, who will they turn to? You.

Today your clients are still employed. They might tell you, "Oh, all my benefits information is online." Your response? "I'll tell you what, we will print out a copy and keep a copy here. Do you know why? Because when they let you go, the first thing they will do is disconnect you from the server. In fact, that's exactly how you know you are no longer with the corporation!"

Check for In-Service Withdrawals

Once you get the summary plan description, look for *in-service withdrawals*. That means your clients have the opportunity to take withdrawals from an employer-sponsored retirement plan while still employed, once they reach retirement age, based on the plan document. In-service withdrawal provisions will allow clients to take money out of the retirement plan and put it into an IRA. Why would you as CRO recommend that? Why would your clients want to do that? One word, Enron. Enron represents an emotional touchstone for an entire generation of people. It says, "I can lose the most important assets I have through no fault of my own. I don't trust management anymore."

As CRO, in-service withdrawals are one more way you can provide service to your clients to help them reach their financial milestones (59 1/2, 62, and 100). By moving some of their retirement money to a retirement account with their CRO, what are the chances that the rest of the money will follow?

Get the Retirement Plan Statement

When you meet with your clients, make sure they bring their retirement plan statement. This is an opportunity to review asset allocations, an exercise that becomes especially important as the number of retirement and other investment accounts increases. Someone has to look at the client's big picture. As CRO, that's your job.

Reviewing the retirement plan statement also allows you to check to see if there's any company stock in the retirement account. If so, be aware of special rules that apply, which are related to *net unrealized appreciation (NUA)*. If company stock is in the plan, there is *not* a 20 percent withholding on the fair market value of the stock. Deliver the stock to the individual and she will pay income tax on the cost basis (provided by the company). The individual will then pay long-term capital gains when the stock is sold.

Get Copies of the Plan's Correspondence

Next, ask clients to send you any and all correspondence they receive from their retirement plans. With mergers, plan revisions, and the generally increasing velocity of change, chances are the amount of information your client gets—and will pass along—will increase at a dramatic pace. Learning about a company merger or buyout can be another venue for providing service to your clients.

Suppose the client's employer, Company B, is bought out by another company, Company A, by whom your client will now be employed. Thanks to the repeal of the *Same Desk Rule* beginning in 2002, your client may now be eligible to take a distribution from the Company B retirement plan (if the employer allows it) by satisfying the "severance from employment" requirement. (Note: Before 2002, if Company A bought Company B, and the employee of Company B stayed on with Company A, that person was *not* eligible for a distribution.) It's an opportunity for the employee, your client, to take more control over the retirement fund assets.

What you are doing now—while your client is gainfully employed—is laying the groundwork to become the person with the information they need at the point they need information and advice. It's very much like the phone systems that inform you that your call is being answered by Audix. Who *is* Audix?[2] Unless you're in the market for a large phone system, you won't care. At some point your clients will be in the middle of a stressful decision-making process, and they will remember these conversations. Your CRO services will be like the Audix message to someone who really needs a new phone system. Who will they call to help them? It's going to be their CRO who has copies of all their company's retirement plan paperwork!

Get the IRA—Get All the IRAs

Since we've been talking about people who are already your clients, you probably have at least one of their IRAs. How do you know if there are more IRAs? Think about the number of times your clients have called to find out what your IRA is paying. This means there is another one somewhere else.

As CRO, when you encounter questions like this, you have a great opportunity to start questioning your client about beneficiaries. Naming a beneficiary can be a complicated planning issue, as we discuss later. But as a start, you want to make sure that the client doesn't still list the beneficiary as the ex-wife from the divorce ten years ago. You can also ask about beneficiaries for those "other IRAs." You might also ask, "Wouldn't it be easier to oversee your retirement investments if you had them all in one place?" In fact, the beneficiary update call is a service call that you need to make annually.

Every CRO needs the client's IRA as a landing pad for all the potential rollover assets—both with the thought that this will be the IRA that all others are consolidated into, and that this is the account that will accept company retirement plan rollovers. IRAs represent one of the fastest-growing segments of the U.S. retirement market in the past ten years. According to the Investment Company Institute, IRAs made up $2.5 trillion in assets of the $11 trillion dollar U.S. retirement market by year-end 2001—nearly a quarter of the market.[3]

The Rollover Magnet

A study by the Financial Research Corporation (FRC) estimated that assets in annual rollovers were on track to reach $260 billion by the end of 2002. What's more, the market is expected to grow to $420 billion in annual rollovers for 2006. That translates to an estimated $1.7 trillion in rollover activity for the five-year period of 2002-2006.[4]

At some point, all workers will retire from the work force. Although that's important, a study by the Investment Company Institute showed that in any given year, around 75 percent of all rollovers come from job changers. Many workers will change jobs during their career—and may do so frequently, according to statistics from the Department of Labor. The study showed that on average, workers change jobs nearly every four years, and will need to decide what to do with their money from their employer's plan.[5]

That means that up to 25 percent of your existing client base could be eligible for a rollover in any given year—putting the rollover opportunity right in your own backyard.

Studies have repeatedly shown that people tend to bring their distribution to the person who has their IRA instead of keeping it with the company that administered their retirement plans. An FRC study of Power Boomers showed that respondents rated their level of satisfaction with retirement plan providers much lower than those handling their retail and IRA accounts.[6] The key to success may be to get to the investor first—and early on.

The legislation we talked about earlier, EGTRRA, has made the IRA the primary retirement vehicle. It raised the limit on IRA contributions and also made it possible to roll over any retirement plan to an IRA.

The Baby Boom generation is accumulating its wealth primarily in retirement plans sponsored by their employers as well as in their IRAs. During the asset accumulation phase that most of the Boomers have been in, the concepts for these tax-deferred vehicles have been pretty simple: contribute and take full advantage of the plan. Financial advisors have added value by recommending the allocation of the assets. All that is changing as the Baby Boom generation heads to retirement. They and their advisors are facing a whole new set of issues. The value-added of the financial services industry will be the ability to understand the needs of clients and guide them through the maze of procedures to access their retirement money. See Figure 9.1 for a quick summary of how IRA assets are treated differently than other assets.

Many individuals believe that they—not the government or other sources—are responsible for their own retirement. In 1999, an AARP study conducted by RoperASW showed that over 80 percent of individuals surveyed (2,001 American adults between the ages of 33 and 52) thought so.[7] Here are some findings that demonstrate many Baby Boomers believe they will be the only ones funding their retirement:

• 60 percent are counting on savings and investments to provide their retirement income.

- 68 percent believe they can count on self-directed sources of income like *IRAs* and 401(k)s.

- 70 percent state that they will do everything they can to avoid depending on their children for financial help during retirement (and only nine percent think it's even fair to ask their children for financial help).

- Only 48 percent think that they can count on Social Security as an additional source of retirement income.[8]

FIGURE 9.1   **Eight Ways IRA Assets Are Different from Other Assets**

1. An IRA is a contract, and the death benefits pass by contract (IRA benefits do not pass via the will, no matter what the will says).

2. IRA assets do not receive a step-up in cost basis at the death of the owner.

3. IRA assets do not receive the favorable capital gains treatment when liquidated.

4. IRAs cannot be transferred to a living trust during the IRA owner's life.

5. IRAs cannot be gifted to heirs during the IRA owner's life. Any change of ownership results in a distribution (a taxable event).

6. IRA distributions (lifetime versus death) follow different rules.

7. IRA distributions do not have any IRS published forms to simply complete, unlike almost all other tax-law requirements.

8. IRAs' death distributions require a specialized plan separate from, but coordinated with, the client's estate plan.

Then Consider Roth IRA

No discussion of IRAs would be complete without the Roth IRA. The Roth IRA, named after former Senator William V. Roth, Jr., was created as a result of the Taxpayer Relief Act of 1997. The main advantages of the Roth IRA are that the earnings escape being taxed and minimum distribution rules do not apply. If clients are able to live on other resources after retirement, they do not have to draw on Roth IRAs at age 70 1/2. That means earnings continue to grow tax-free. The drawback of those advantages is that taxpayers cannot take a tax deduction upon making the contribution to Roth IRAs.

So which is more important? It depends on the situation, and assumptions about the future. When will clients need to withdraw money from the Roth IRA? What will the tax bracket be then? What will the Roth earn? There are calculators galore on the Internet to run an analysis, but the rule of thumb is that most people are better off contributing to a Roth IRA than a traditional IRA. See Chapter 15, *Continuing Your Education as CRO*, for a more detailed discussion of the nuts and bolts of Roth IRAs, including the age-old CRO question: how, and when should a client convert from a traditional IRA to a Roth IRA?

IRA Beneficiary Dilemmas

You should prepare clients to give careful thought about whom they name as a beneficiary of their IRA and retirement plan. Will they be creating a legacy or an estate tax liability? In the context of whom they wish to receive the assets, clients may think the answers are simple. However, deciding on the most effective strategy may not be quite as straightforward.

Individual Retirement Answers

Use the following questions as a starting point to open this conversation with your clients:

1. Does your spouse need the money for support if he or she survives you?

2. If you leave the IRA to children or grandchildren, you need to consider these questions: "What will they do with the money?" and, "What will the money do to them?"

3. If you leave the IRA to your children or grandchildren, how will they handle taxes owed?

4. How do you divide assets among children? Equal amounts? Each according to individual needs?

5. Might this be a good asset to leave to your church or favorite charity?

6. Have you considered the benefits of leaving the IRA in a trust rather than leaving it to any particular person?

While taxes are always a concern, do not let your clients get caught in the trap of selecting their beneficiaries solely for tax reasons. In the pecking order of estate planning issues, taxes should not be the first consideration in making decisions. Other issues take precedence. For example, naming a child or grandchild as a beneficiary may be a great tax idea; however, such beneficiaries may not place the same value on money and savings as the IRA owner. They may want the money today! Upon the death of the account owner, the beneficiary has the right to withdraw all of the money. In addition, creditors can access the IRA or it can be split in a divorce. Instead, consider naming a trust for the child or grandchild as beneficiary, and appointing a trustee. This can prevent these unintended consequences yet still allow access to the money.

If a grandchild or a trust for a grandchild is named beneficiary, the IRA is subject to the 50 percent Generation-Skipping Transfer Tax. If the IRA is significant in size, consider obtaining life insurance. A life insurance trust, properly structured to match the distribution provisions of the rest of your estate, is clearly the best way to own life insurance. The proceeds are used to pay the estate taxes on the IRA.

Deciding who to name as beneficiary of an IRA or a retirement plan is a major planning decision. Most people don't take the time necessary to do correct planning. No matter whom your clients have already named or what mistakes they might have made, chances are very good that if you are talking to a client, those mistakes can still be corrected. Coordinate the strategies with a knowledgeable attorney to figure out the right answer for your client. We'll talk more about coordinating your clients' team of experts in Chapter 11, *Defining Your Role as CRO*.

For a story that illustrates all the IRA considerations and complications, see Chapter 12, *The IRA Beneficiary Dilemma*. There you'll meet John and Lynne who face a millionaire couple's estate problem—although they hardly feel like millionaires. The key lesson to learn from John and Lynne's saga is to have this IRA beneficiary conversation with your clients sooner rather than later. It's also critical to revisit the conversation every year, since births, deaths, divorces, and life's shake-ups can dramatically change the family landscape and reshape your clients' thinking about who-gets-what and how-will-they get-it. Figure 9.2 is a handy way to remember what you need to do.

```
┌─────────────────────────────────────────────────────────────┐
│ FIGURE 9.2    The CRO's "CYA" Protects You and Your Clients  │
├─────────────────────────────────────────────────────────────┤
```

- **Check the IRA custodian to ensure beneficiaries on file are correct.**
  With mergers of financial institutions or even transfers of the accounts
  from one custodian to another, forms can be misplaced. Do not assume
  that everything is in order just because it was the last time you checked.

- **Set up yearly meetings to ensure beneficiaries are correct.**
  Situations change, and marriages, divorces, births, and deaths affect
  clients and beneficiaries. If a child is a beneficiary and that child is
  going through a divorce, you may find that an ex-in-law has rights
  to the assets.

- **Secure acknowledged receipts of beneficiary designations.**
  FedEx, UPS, DHL, etc. all require receipts, most timed and signed.
  Copies of these belong in the client's file. If the IRA custodian loses
  the originals, the institution's default policy will govern distributions
  to your client's beneficiaries.

CRO's Opportunities When Clients Take Action

By being proactive and preparing your clients for *The Winds of Change*, and
by making it easy and non-threatening for them to take action before they are
downsized, you are positioning yourself as a trusted expert, their CRO. You are
creating the building blocks for helping your clients through one of the most
stressful events of their work life.

During a stressful decision-making process, people always turn to those
whom they believe have the most information. If you've told the story and helped
them to take action, your clients will perceive you as a knowledgeable resource
who can help them through the challenging times. You will have one or more of
their IRAs, ready to accept a rollover from a company plan. You will have their
summary plan description and be able to navigate the shoals of funds transfer.
You will be on top of current correspondence. You may even be able to help them
with in-service withdrawals, or net unrealized appreciation, depending on what
they hold in their company plans. Best of all, your clients have confirmed their
commitment to getting your help by taking actions now that will enable you to
help them when they really need it. Of course it's also key to build the right group
of people—your ideal clients. We'll talk next about defining and finding your
ideal clients.

Chapter 10

DEFINING AND FINDING THE IDEAL CLIENT

"Smart and experienced brokers/advisers have learned that you must be selective about the types of clients you want to attract...You need to communicate in a way that reveals your principles regarding long-term investing."[1]
- Scott West & Mitch Anthony, *StorySelling for Financial Advisors*

A Macro Perspective: Who Will Our Clients Be?

Finding ideal clients starts with being aware of the larger social and economic changes affecting the working population.

When manufacturing jobs moved overseas, you probably didn't feel the effects unless one of your clients or a family member was among those who lost a job. We learned that this is how economic growth happens. Now the news of call centers and software-programmers outsourced to India does not feel like "progress." We "knowledge workers" are watching livelihoods jeopardized by the same free-market principles that changed U.S. manufacturing. These days, white-collar jobs are as vulnerable to overseas migration as any other. If finance, accounting, and engineering-design jobs are moved offshore, what can't be moved?

Creative destruction of jobs is not news. Every economic era has seen massive displacement of workers, families, and entire industries. Still, not everything can be outsourced. Despite the Internet, videoconferencing, and cell phones, plenty of jobs—even well paying jobs—require face-to-face contact. Society cannot function without doctors, police officers, or judges. So the economy will continue to need trainers, researchers, economists, teachers, lawyers, editors, and executives to manage them all.

Remember that work will always be here because "here" is where workers want to be. The U.S. remains the world's top destination spot for both well-off immigrants and refugees seeking economic prosperity. The U.S. still has the competitive advantage of creativity, innovative thinking, and invention.

Sorting for Workplace Winners

In this high-stakes, globalized workplace, who will win—and become a prospect for you as CRO? Where will the high-paying jobs come from? The talk at the start of the "Internet economy" was that the Internet was going to eliminate intermediaries; the path would go directly from producer to consumer. This might have been a misjudgment. Intermediaries survive by adding value. It is not that we do not need middlemen—we just need different kinds of middlemen—and that's where the new jobs will be. *A good example is the value-added services that you, as CRO, bring to your client relationships versus the less customized services people get through "online brokerages" or investing directly in big mutual fund companies.*

America's economy is essentially talent-driven. We talked earlier about free agent, project-based workers. Remember the five minutes of credits that run at the end of current movies? The teams come together to make the film or do the trade show. They bring expertise and staff from a wide range of arenas. When one project is complete, they disperse until the next one. The real winners in this job market will be highly talented and entrepreneurial individuals who know where and how to market their skills and accomplishments to employers and team builders. Their talents are sought-after and rewarded accordingly.

Look for individuals who see their work lives not as jobs but as a series of risk-management choices. It is important for workers not to leave their careers in their employers' hands. Everyone now has the responsibility to maintain a high personal skill level. Most people have not accepted that level of personal responsibility. Both you and your clients will need to create work/life plans in which the bar for excellence is constantly being raised.

From a Company Perspective

As employers turn payroll from a "fixed" to "variable" cost, economic risks shift to workers. What might employment look like for your client? Those who are full-time employees will increasingly see their income depend more on commissions and performance bonuses. They may be a partner in an entrepreneurial group whose profits vary. They may work in a professional-services firm, doing client projects for a percentage of overall earnings. Maybe they'll be talent for an agency or temp firm that posts for a limited time or to a specific project and takes a percentage of earnings in return. Or perhaps they are the free agents selling services to the highest bidder. Your clients may experience any and all of the above work/pay combinations at one time or another.

Not every company will be forced to change the way it does business. There are plenty of old-style, "mom and pop" organizations or niche businesses that are thriving. The fastest growing segment of employment in the United States will be self-employment, including firms under 50 employees. Over 700,000 new businesses were started each year over the last decade.[2] Many of these businesses will continue to generate new jobs every year, although the number of business failures will increase accordingly, especially during the bust cycles of the boom/bust economy. This new entrepreneurship is likely to breed greater innovation, competition, and productivity.

Between 1979 and 1993, Fortune 500 companies reduced their personnel by 4.8 million, while firms with fewer than 500 employees generated 16 million new jobs.[3] Expect this trend to continue. Large Fortune 500 companies, especially service industries, will continue to cut jobs as they attempt to survive intense competition. Learning what it takes to serve this nation of free agents will be a continuing challenge for would-be CROs.

Well over two-thirds of Baby Boomers born between 1946 and 1964, or around 77 million individuals, are potential prospects for a CRO's services. For a more detailed snapshot of Baby Boomers as prospects, see the Appendix for a brief summary and list of the sources. The research indicates that the main concerns of this aging population are, "Not having enough money to do what I want; not being healthy enough to do what I want; and having to go back to work because I will need the money."[4] These are issues that CROs need to be aware of in order to learn what they can recommend to allay these concerns.

Defining Your Ideal Clients

All the business-building books say: find a niche and specialize. Well, I'd like to tell you about a niche that already exists in your book of business: "real people" riches. As the industry focuses on the high net worth client, I would make a case for building your business around the 104 million households that have less than $1 million in investable assets. There are only about 250,000 households that have $5 million in investable assets. I suggest you become the Chief Retirement Officer for your clients first—building up a book of business that reflects those "real people," as well as their friends, neighbors, and industry colleagues.

Your clients' concerns are summed up with one question, *"Can we find financial peace of mind?"* Translated, this means, "Do they have the financial resources to meet their needs?" Their needs range from paying for their children's educations, planning for retirement, and, for many, supporting elderly parents (see Figure 10.1).

FIGURE 10.1	**What do the CRO's prospects worry about?**

Here are the top eight items that a CRO's prospects worry about:

1. How to make it to 59 1/2 (when they can access retirement funds without penalty)

2. How to make it to 62 (when Social Security payments can start)

3. Not knowing if their money will last their entire life (making it to 100)

4. Health care costs

5. Independence

6. Reducing taxes

7. Social Security

8. Employment

What may be most frightening is that many are acting like ostriches, hiding their heads in the sand, financially illiterate. Now, I did not say stupid—and illiterate might be too harsh—"consciously incompetent" might be the phrase. Consciously incompetent means, "I know that a proper diet and exercise are good for me, but eating cookies and watching TV feel so good that I just don't exercise." The underlying feelings of being overwhelmed by change, while trying to meet the demands of both work and family, mean that making financial decisions and taking action seem like hard work. The amount of information seems to be growing, and the rules seem to be changing.

But are the rules changing, or are clients just ignoring them? Your job as a Chief Retirement Officer may be trying to get your clients to do what they *should* do, rather than what they want to do. In fact, your role may be to get them to do the opposite of what they want! They can't send an 18-year-old to college if they use the college money to replace the two-year-old SUV with a bigger one.

The rules for financial success are simple. But it's the kind of simplicity that lies beyond sophistication. For example, understanding that information is not wisdom; or that emotions, not intellect, are making many of the decisions; or that discipline can be hard. So unless you as the CRO give them a process, unfortunately, many will receive an unpleasant financial wake up call when, out of nowhere, they get "the package."

"Real People" Riches

A common rule of thumb is that 80 percent of your business comes from 20 percent of your book. What if you could make the rest of your clients as productive—even half as productive—as your top 20 percent? If you haven't systematically worked that part of your book of business, now is the time to put in the effort. And it beats cold calls.

If you don't yet specialize in helping *all* your clients with IRA rollovers, the place to start is right in your book. Earlier we mentioned statistics that, between early retirement, downsizing, and general job changes and promotions, easily a quarter of the working population changes companies every year. These events create opportunities when "the money is in motion." Even if the rollover from company plans to IRA is modest—in the five-figures or low six-figures—the ongoing growth in those accounts coupled with continued job mobility means that you have a viable opportunity to provide a service to your clients as their CRO.

Start today to avoid the syndrome "I" call, "I didn't know you did that." If you have a client who doesn't know you do rollovers, then you won't get their IRA rollover, and you won't get their referrals. Make sure you communicate this specialty proactively and often—after all, you're a CRO!

As you focus on the niche of clients who are in your book of business, and let them know that you specialize in IRA rollovers, you will be in a position to leverage those relationships. Diligently and consistently ask for referrals. Ask current clients for the trends in their fields, industries, and companies. Find out if their company may be downsizing or outsourcing. Will there be a group of people you can help? Build those connections with clients' friends, neighbors, and colleagues. Some clients, whose workplaces are in the throes of change, may even help you by referring you to the Human Resources department in their company. There, you may be able to provide informational rollover seminars to a whole group of people who will be getting "the package." For more marketing ideas, see Chapter 14, *Growing Your Retirement Business*.

Discovering and Naming Your Ideal Client

As you're making the pass through your book, revisiting your clients' workplaces and industries, you may start to notice a pattern. Who are the people in your top 20 percent? Are they in similar industries? Are they at a certain level of position within their organizations? Tease out the patterns to uncover the characteristics that make a great client *for you*. Then the goal is to prospect in such a way that you find more of those winners.

In my travels and visits with some of the top producing financial professionals in the country, I've seen all kinds of specialties. A few years ago, the ideal client was the 63-year-old retiree from the phone company. As food for thought, here are a few of the varieties of focuses for financial practices I've come across:

- Focus on retirees from a particular company.

- Focus on higher-level people downsized from a company—those with at least $500,000 in the package and stock options.

- Focus on an industry (pilots, doctors, aerospace workers who were in the military prior to their business career, teachers, etc.).

- Focus on executives that relocate to your area.

- Focus on franchises and entrepreneurs.

The goal is to become a specialist in an area, industry, occupation, or even in a specific company. As you review who's who in your book of business, you will start to see the kind of clients you covet. You'll see the specialties emerge: oil industry, shipbuilding, or individuals such as accountants or factory floor supervisors. Becoming a specialist to this group (or groups) means you have identified your niche. Ideally this will lead to your clients referring colleagues who are similarly employed and who need similar types of retirement solutions.

The key then is to increase your audience of likely prospects in that target niche. What do they want? Are they really a good fit? Pick the one group that is best suited to you. Write a phrase describing your target group. For example, "I'd like to be the Chief Retirement Officer for high-technology professionals in the Boston area." Remember: the narrower the niche, the better.

With this in mind, list a couple of criteria you believe are most important about your ideal client. This benchmark will enable you to make decisions about those you will accept as clients and how much time and effort you are willing to invest in those relationships. By working with more "ideal" clients, you should expect better quality relationships, better control over your time, and increased revenue.

For example, "I would like clients who...

• need, appreciate, and are willing to pay for services."

• have the resources and are motivated to take control of their financial lives."

• take a long-term approach to investments."

• are willing to give referrals."

Identify your top ten prospective clients. What differentiates you from those with whom they are doing business? Competition is a sign that there are opportunities for success.

Interview people from possible prospect groups. Ask them about their goals and their experience with financial services. Be candid about your intentions, and see if their responses match your assumptions about them.

Get answers to these questions for yourself in going through this process:.

1. Can I offer the services they need?

2. Am I comfortable working with these types of individuals?

3. Does their investment history suggest that I will be able to meet my income goals?

4. Do they offer the potential for referral business?

5. Will I be able to service the clients I might acquire?

Finding and Building Your Targeted Niche of Ideal Prospects

Becoming a CRO specializing in IRA rollovers and company distributions is one of the first steps in creating your specialty. Following that, identify the industry or group of professionals for whom you especially want to provide CRO services. We will focus on some business-building ideas that have been successful for other financial professionals as they uncover more of their ideal clients.

Keep in mind that knowledge is power when it comes to capturing your share of the rollover market. Many clients and prospects look to their financial professional for guidance on how best to handle a distribution from their old plan. As a CRO, it's critical that you understand the client distribution questions and issues listed below in Figure 10.2.

FIGURE 10.2	**Eight Client Distribution Questions— and Two Key Issues**

1. Is there a distributable event?

2. What distribution options are allowed for by the plan?

3. Some distribution decisions are irrevocable.
   Does this one fall into that category?

4. What are the plan's investment options?

5. Are there employer securities?

6. Can the plan investments be rolled over in kind?

7. Does the plan allow for loans?

8. Who is the beneficiary on the account?

9. This may be the largest sum of money your client ever sees.

10. This may be a stressful time for many people.
    They are looking for guidance and advice.[5]

New Employee, Old Distribution

New employees face choices, choices, and more choices. In addition to choices about health care in the new company plan, there's FSA, AD&D, disability, life insurance packages, and of course, what to do with the money in the retirement plan of their prior company. By focusing on new employees and relocating employees, you can bring your expertise at IRA Rollovers to their aid. Because their choice can trigger tax consequences or early distribution penalties, they are prime candidates to seek out financial advice. Rolling their old retirement monies into an IRA not only helps them avoid taxes and penalties on their distribution, but also gives them the flexibility to choose where and how their money will be invested.

You can work to capture these key prospects through your referral network by asking clients, "Are there any new people at your firm who have come from another organization? Perhaps I can help them with an IRA Rollover from their prior company." Current clients may also be helpful in providing a copy of the internal company newsletter, in which newly hired staff are often welcomed to the organization, or even a company directory to help you contact their colleagues. You can also keep tabs on new movers and shakers by following the "Who's Moving Up" sections in the local papers and in industry trade and professional journals.

Also in the business of connecting people to new companies are temporary agencies and headhunters, also known as executive recruiters. You'll even find that these agencies specialize. Get to know the firms that specialize in your niche. Some firms focus on CFOs, some on marketing personnel, some in the high tech industry. Once you've identified a potential niche, get to know the other kinds of professionals serving that market, and build your relationships with firms that already specialize in working with that population. By creating alliances with these hiring professionals and organizations, you will be able to provide for them an additional valuable service they wouldn't normally be able to offer their clients—such as financial seminars and information on rollovers. In addition, you are prospecting in a fertile and largely untapped arena.

Offer Rollover Informational Seminars

With these outside groups, as well as within an organization, maximize your time by meeting as many prospects at one time as you can when you host a rollover seminar. The seminar format provides the educational platform that assures your credibility. At the same time, it gives you a chance to present yourself, your CRO credentials, and the tremendous services you can offer to the prospects. You can illustrate your experience, trustworthiness, and ability to help them protect their assets. From the seminar attendees, you can invite appointments for one-on-one conversations.

Tap Into Layoffs

Ideally your current clients may be among the first to let you know that layoffs are in the offing at their firm or in their industry. In addition, there are other avenues for gathering information about downsizings and layoffs.

If you can build a relationship with the Human Resources people at targeted companies within your niche, you are positioning your CRO services for helping them educate those who will be "getting the package." Ideally, you want to provide educational seminars outlining the possibilities for what people can do in this situation, as opposed to selling specific products at this stage. Providing valuable information, as opposed to a sales pitch, will go a long way to solidifying your credibility as CRO (Remember, educate first and sell later).

Sometimes it's not the Human Resource department that sees the need for educational services for downsized employees. Sometimes it's the business leaders or decision-makers. They may realize that their people could use some help going through a difficult transition. Networking with these people, often entrepreneurs, company founders, CFOs and the like, is another way to provide your value-added CRO services for their people.

Some advisors have suggested a "diplomatic intelligence" method for collecting information regarding who is coming and going at an organization. You won't always be able to access critical information from those in charge. They may not even know the details you need. Instead, infiltrate the organization and get to know the real people who have access to the information—names, dates, data— you need. Secretaries and administrative assistants, factory floor workers, and shift supervisors are all potential sources for tracking those joining the organization or leaving, who's getting close to retiring, and potential outsourcing of whole departments.

Your contact inside a company may also be aware of a future layoff, and the outplacement firm that will get the contract to help displaced workers. That outplacement firm is another organization with whom it makes sense to network, with the goal of creating a strategic alliance. Such firms often get paid based on how many people show up on a given day. If you offer to conduct a "Rollover Seminar" for their clients, you win, by getting to present your educational offering and credentials to a prime audience of prospects. The outplacement firm wins because a seminar will likely draw a significant audience of people actually coming in that day. And, the workers win because they learn about their financial options. The more creatively you can think for prospecting scenarios that provide a "win" for all involved, the faster your pool of prospects will grow.

Opportunities to Connect with Ideal Clients and Prospects

Working with a CRO means your clients and prospects can start to develop peace of mind connected with most, if not all, of the financial-related issues that cause concern. With your help, they will be able to take a long, hard look at their financial reality. Workplace and retirement issues are of critical importance.

Ideally, as you specialize in a niche, you will bring the added value of a deep understanding of the company, industry, or niche you've identified.

As you define your ideal clients and then find more prospects in whatever industry niche you choose, you'll be focusing your strategy on "real people" riches. This is an opportunity to build your CRO practice aggressively from your current book of clients, knowing that millions share similar financial concerns. In addition, you will position yourself to take advantage of targeted referrals. You can practice outside-the-box prospecting strategies to further grow a pool of the most promising prospects.

As we move on, we will address how you will define your role as CRO, then uncover answers to the most plaguing question of all, "How will my clients make it to 59 1/2, 62, and 100?"

Chapter 11

DEFINING YOUR ROLE AS CRO: THE CRO ORGANIZER

"Work like hell and wear a red shirt."
  – Railroad Baron when asked by a common worker on how to stand out among thousands of other workers.

  "I went to my doctor's appointment last week. After escorting me into the examination room, Dr. Jones proceeded to tell me all about himself: where he grew up, went to college, and attended medical school. He described his internship, highlighted the qualifications of his nurses and support staff, and mentioned his new X-ray machine. He then started a PowerPoint presentation with eye-catching graphics and charts that told me all about the wonderful services that he and his staff provided. He even included several patient testimonials. After about 45 minutes, the doctor asked me how I felt. I said I twisted my ankle playing with the kids last weekend, and so he wrapped it, gave me a prescription, and sent me on my way."

The Case of the Wrong Story

What's wrong with this story? Doctors don't work that way. They ask questions. Even before you see a doctor, you fill out a medical history form. They want to know about your ailments, illnesses, and injuries. They want to know if you are allergic to any drugs or if you have seen other physicians. When doctors come in and begin their examination, they hit you with more questions. Depending on your answers, they may perform various tests: blood pressure, urine analysis, X-rays, EKG. Based on the results of those tests, they may ask you more questions and/or run still more tests to find out what you need.

Does my tale of Dr. Jones sound strangely familiar? It should. Based on what I've seen, this kind of presentation happens every day. It sounds suspiciously like the approach that the vast majority of financial advisors use when they're prospecting. How do they ever make a client diagnosis if they're doing all the talking? You don't do that, right?

Take a lesson from visiting your doctor. Questions are the way to uncover the financial ailments and issues your clients and prospects have. Asking questions is the most valuable time you spend with clients. It is also the first key to distinguish you, as CRO, from the army of aggressive competitors you face in the financial advice business.

Think about your circle of prospects and contacts in which you search for new clients. Within that circle, how many financial advisors are competing with you? Twenty? Fifty? One hundred? Competition in the financial services industry is fierce, and it's getting more intense. You need to use a clear position to develop an image that people will remember. A good position is clear, concise, and easy for prospects to understand.

As CRO, You Offer a Proven Process

Positioning yourself as the client's Chief Retirement Officer creates a unique identity that gives clients a lasting impression—one they will identify only with you. It is a way for you distinguish yourself in a crowded field, be remembered, and stand out from your competitors.

Have you ever known any individuals who were very good at doing something they really didn't like? Without the power of belief in the work of wealth-building and helping to create someone's retirement dream, you cannot succeed. CROs should believe passionately in the importance of what they do. Knowledge can never account for all your success. What really moves people is your belief in your work and the passion you bring to building relationships and creating winning retirements for your clients. I believe that a Chief Retirement Officer can do more good for more people and can make that good last far longer than almost any other profession.

One of the basic purposes of a Chief Retirement Officer is to anticipate scenarios that could financially impair your clients' futures and use financial products to protect against catastrophic loss. The service is to build and maintain long-term, value-added sales- and service-oriented business relationships with clients. As

CRO, your "product" is yourself.

But what does a Chief Retirement Officer actually do? A CRO's duties include planning, and continually reviewing and evaluating investment performance of available resources used during a specific established schedule of retirement. The CRO evaluates financial systems to provide reasonable assurance that obligations and costs during retirement are covered. The CRO provides centralized services for scheduling of and disbursement of assets. The CRO serves as principal advisor to the client in matters relating to financial and resources management focused on retirement.

The Six-Step CRO Process

Being a CRO is a multi-faceted role. By looking at the activities in an organized, comprehensive CRO process, you will help your clients see the value you can provide. The following six-step process covers the ground a CRO needs to address:

1. Ask questions that uncover concerns and make connections that create a memorable experience (identify the puzzle pieces).

2. Get the IRA as a landing pad for further asset collection and growth (See Chapter 9, *How to Get Your Clients to Take Action*).

3. Grasp the big picture when you get all the information in your CRO-Client Organizer.

4. Allocate assets, manage risks, and explain approaches that are solutions to clients' needs.

5. Lead the client's strategic personal finance team (attorney, accountant, real estate professional, banker, etc.).

6. Continue ongoing planning in the context of appropriate asset disbursement.

CROs work with their clients to develop a mission statement, a written business and investment plan, and short-, medium-, and long-term goals. This information is based on extensive questioning and open-ended explorations of clients' life purposes and missions: the accomplishment they want to make in their lives; and the legacy they want to leave and to whom. As part of the client's "Annual Review and Financial Check-up," be sure to check these documents for any necessary changes or revisions.

Clients Seek Memorable Experiences from Service Providers

The customer experience is key to success in securing a competitive advantage in today's buyers' markets. Young people buy products. Middle age and older people buy experiences. Marketing is not about getting out facts but about stimulating emotional centers of the brain. Creating customer experiences that give a competitive edge isn't necessarily expensive or complicated. The shift from a product- to customer-centered mindset changes how we view marketing and customers. For example:

- Customers are no longer targets; they are humans to be served.

- Marketing is no longer a game of persuasion; it is a service.

- The focus is no longer on products; it is on the customer's experience.

Top salespeople have always personalized the customer experience. Only recently have marketers begun thinking about personalization as a marketing strategy.

Don't tell Lexus that older people won't switch brands! Many former loyal Mercedes and Cadillac owners will now be Lexus owners for the rest of their lives—provided Lexus continues to deliver on the customer experience. Lexus turned enough prospects into loyal customers by establishing connections with them to earn the highest repurchase rates in the auto industry.

Perhaps no company has reflected better understanding of the midlife soul in its marketing than the company New Balance. It became the fastest growing shoe company in America by connecting with the more temperate behavior of the Baby Boomers with its tagline, "Achieve new balance."

In *Toward a Psychology of Being,* Maslow said that mature people reflect "polarities and oppositions" in behavior. They strive to simplify their lives; experience changes in values; become more autonomous; and avoid extremes.[1]

"Know your customer" is the first commandment of our business. To "know your customer" includes understanding that a 56-year-old is not just a 30-year older version of a 26-year-old self. Midlife changes to the Baby Boomers should change the approach of your marketing.

Up until now, marketers have said, "Sell using a rational marketing approach. Recite product features and functional benefits, handle objections, and close." Joe Pine and Jim Gilmore in *The Experience Economy* basically declared product-centered marketing dead. Like many others, Pine and Gilmore say marketing is now more about the customer experience than the product.[2]

Rational marketing works better among the young because the young want proof. The older mind often tunes out bold, absolute claims about products and companies. The Baby Boomers will respond quite favorably to companies that see them as whole people, not merely as prospects for a product or service.

Focus on Creating Outstanding Client Experiences

If you really want to set your CRO practice apart, let me make two recommendations. First, learn the art of *StorySelling*, which is from the book, *StorySelling for Financial Advisors*, written by Scott West and Mitch Anthony. Get it, read it, and use the concepts in every client meeting. It's an incredibly effective process that shows financial professionals how to use the stories and metaphors clients can relate to in order to help them understand retirement and investing concepts that seem foreign or complex. Find the gold mines and avoid the land mines.

You should also check out *The New Retirementality* by Mitch Anthony. For many, retirement may become one of the longest periods in their lives. How people spend their "golden years" should reflect their goals, values, and interests. To truly move your CRO practice in the direction of seeing and addressing your clients as "whole people" (as they want to be known and addressed), this book offers a bigger picture that will dramatically distinguish you and your practice from the competition. You're still the CRO; your focus remains on their financial picture; but you work with them in the largest, most spacious concept of what their retirement lives are all about.

Putting Together the Puzzle

Your clients are hardworking people, many of whom are overwhelmed by the pace of change and the extensive, ever-growing "to do" lists that spring up in their PDAs, on the refrigerator, in organizers, on calendars, and on a flurry of yellow sticky notes around the car, house, and office. Many of these people would gladly pay for help because they're so busy. They can see it would be money well spent—if only they knew what they needed!

When it comes to financial issues relating to retirement, they are usually holding quite a few pieces of the puzzle. They may have an IRA, and there's the employer retirement plan for both working spouses. They may have life insurance and workplace health insurance. They have a couple of small accounts started for the kids' college education. The result? They have the puzzle pieces without the picture on the box. As a CRO, you have access to the big picture—the puzzle box lid with the picture on it. What you don't necessarily know are the puzzle pieces your clients already have. That's when the financial organizer becomes the tool of choice and a way to save anguish for you and your clients.

The Retirement Organizer: Make Sure You Have the Information You Need

Let's say you have at least one of your clients' IRAs. In Chapter 9, *How to Get Clients to Take Action*, we talked about getting all the IRAs and all the paperwork from the workplace retirement plan. These items are an integral part of your CRO-Client Organizer.

Let me tell you a story of two deaths. Before my father died, he showed me a file labeled W.I.D. in a file cabinet in his office. W.I.D. stood for "When I Die." In one convenient location, he had a list of key advisors and an inventory of important documents we would need.

Recently when my wife's uncle died, I got the job of sorting through the paperwork to figure out where everything was. We first created a list: the what and the where. What accounts are with a broker or an insurance agent? What is the name of the mutual fund company? Is there a safety deposit box? Are there certificates of deposit? Who with? When do they mature? Those were the obvious first categories and places to look. Annuities, IRAs, and retirement plans eventually will send statements. But what about old stock certificates? What about the limited partnership that he didn't talk about? Didn't he have a coin collection?

If you have ever had to deal with the financial aftermath of a loved one's death, you know how important a W.I.D. file is. One of the easiest, earliest, and most critical value-added activities for a CRO is to work with clients to create their W.I.D. file. You can call it your "CRO-Client Retirement Organizer." I've seen dozens of methods for keeping important papers together and gathering a list of financial data that may reside only in your client's head. See Figure 11.1 for the top ten items that should be in the organizer.

For example, if your client has online banking or bill paying, where are the logon and passwords kept? What are they? In our increasingly technological society, that kind of information may only be available in their personal memory. The CRO-Client Organizer is a safe place to "download" such information. Needless to say, it should be updated regularly.

As CRO, you need the CRO-Client Organizer right from the beginning and at every step along the way. Consider the following situations:

FIGURE 11.1	The Retirement Organizer—Top Ten List

At the very least, make sure these ten items
are detailed in the Organizer

1. Contacts list
2. Mutual funds
3. Investments
4. Banks
5. Mortgages, loans
6. Retirement plans
7. Life insurance
8. Corporate benefits
9. Annuities
10. Trusts, financial plan

- *During retirement planning*, the information in a CRO-Client Organizer will help you create strategy, shape portfolios, confirm or revise asset allocations, and list all current holdings.

- *During distribution planning*, the CRO-Client Organizer is the place to collect documents describing benefits, deadlines, and contacts. As it becomes time to start taking distributions from retirement plans, the CRO needs to have access to the big picture, all the requirements, and all the resources.

- *At death*, the CRO-Client Organizer will help bereaved family members deal with the financial issues in an organized fashion. The deceased will have done what he or she could to preserve the peace of mind of the family who will be coping in so many different ways. All too often, only the deceased knows the location of documents related to the financial assets within the estate. With the organizer, that information will be accessible to you as CRO and to the family and beneficiaries.

As the CRO you need to keep copies of your clients' important papers. Fire damages or destroys nearly 2,000 homes every day in the U.S. The last thing your clients need is to have their organized records reduced to ashes. Many lawyers, when they draw up a will, encourage clients to take a copy and leave the signed original in their law offices. After all, the lawyers will need the original when the time comes to file their documents.

Most of the major financial firms provide some kind of Client Information Organizer. We don't have to reinvent the wheel. Use the tools your firm provides. In fact, one advisor found his firm's organizer a real boon for his business. In the newly redesigned organizer his firm created, there were some new tabs. One was for Long-Term Care, and another for Catastrophic Risk. By having a tab, the advisor had a reason to introduce a discussion of catastrophic risk and to talk to clients about long-term care, and their plans for covering the potential risks. Prior to this, he had rarely sold any long-term care insurance. Once he began using the tab to introduce the conversation, suddenly his business in that area took off. Now there's something to put behind the tab. The tabs, or categories on your CRO-Client Organizer, will help you remember all the items for which you can provide assistance. As CRO, it's important to leave no stone unturned.

Here's a more exhaustive list of 20 items to include in the CRO-Client Organizer, with additional items for business owners. While some of the items on the list may simply indicate the location of the information, in other cases, you might as well list the details in the organizer to have them readily available.

- Will
- Social Security number
- Prepaid funeral plan (if there is one) and an outline of client's wishes
- Attorney
- Accountant
- Bank (how many accounts, what kind, where, and how much in each)
- Insurance agent/information on all policies
- Retirement accounts/IRAs/401(k)s
- Stocks/bonds/treasury bills
- Safety deposit box location
- Post office box location
- Property (addresses and deeds or mortgage information)

- Keys and access codes for car, garage, and home or building security systems
- Computer logon or security codes (source of bill-paying information, etc.)
- Debts (names of creditors, how much is owed, and how they can be reached)
- Credit card accounts (address, how much owed, and information on any points or rewards accumulated)
- Monthly bills (location of all relevant statements)
- Records of any personal loans (receipts for payments/receipts marked "paid in full")
- Record of personal items on loan
- Debtors (who owes, and the amount owed)

For clients who operate a business, consider including the following:

- Suppliers and vendors (addresses and contact information)
- Marketing agents and distributors
- Insurance agent for the company
- Contact information for line of leadership succession
- Bank contact and accounts
- Company retirement plan representative

Illustrate the Possibilities

Most advisors realize that the services they currently provide clients focus on allocating assets and managing risks. In addition, as CRO, you need to be able to explain strategic retirement approaches that are solutions to client needs.

On your CRO desktop, you have an array of computer programs you can use as modeling tools. You can run detailed scenarios with your clients. You can run the numbers for "worst case scenarios." You also can tell them how long the money will last at various return rates. Playing "what if" with clients can be a valuable and eye-opening experience for them—yet another of your CRO value-added services. Your clients won't take it kindly to learn that, at a healthy and vigorous 79, they have only enough money to last them until they're 80.

Modeling scenarios and running the numbers can be the key to helping clients see that there are variables and flexibility in the planning process. It also shows how their decisions can help or hinder their long-term potential.

Too often, financial advisors calculate the 30-year retirement plan. To quote the inimitable Jeeves, "I could not advise it, sir." As I've emphasized elsewhere, we live in a society where change is constantly accelerating. Using static numbers and assuming certain investment return percentages over 30 years, or inflation over that period, is short-sighted and not in the best interest of your clients. Rather, I recommend a regular succession of rolling "Five-Year Plans" that are updated every year, or at least every two years. Five years is enough of a window to do serious planning, without having to assume unreasonable expectations of stable results in an unstable world.

Manage Risk

Risk is uncertainty about future outcomes and seems to be increasing just by virtue of our being on the planet right now.

Risk management is a process not a program. It is part science and part art—and focuses on human aspects. Perceptions, attitudes, and expectations may be as important as facts. Risk management requires maintaining perspective. It is designed to give your clients the sense of security that comes with having a clearly defined strategy already in place before an unexpected event occurs. Risk management is not only a defensive mechanism, but also an offensive weapon.

For most of us, managing risk happens all the time. We trade risks, whether negotiating work compensations or benefits packages. Some pay a high premium for maximum medical coverage while others gamble on getting sick. Some refinanced and got a 30-year mortgage; others chose an adjustable rate. Some buy cars; others lease. Some people buy and sell stocks; some, bonds—and some do both.

A CRO can assemble an integrated picture of all client risks, upside and downside, those that can be controlled and those that can't, then guide the client to manage them as an entirety. If you can measure the risk, then you can manage it.

To strengthen safety nets, insurance reduces downside risk. Usually people can insure homes, property, health (use of expensive medical resources), and even the future need for nursing home care. Downside risk protection limits potential losses; it sets the floor. However, insuring financial assets may limit upside return as well as downside risk. Your job as CRO is to help your clients distinguish between what makes sense to insure and what to invest for the whole portfolio, given their specific concerns, risk aversion, and so forth.

As CRO, it's important to emphasize net worth, not income. A salary by itself never made anyone wealthy. We need to concentrate on the whole portfolio. The source of client's future wealth is shifting from money earned to money that earns returns. Rename the "nest egg" the "invest egg." IRAs and retirement plans yield future wealth.

Lead the Retirement Team

Since the CRO serves as the primary advisor to clients in financial matters and resource management for retirement, that means coordinating with an accountant for tax purposes and with a lawyer on wills and trusts. Minimally, these two basic relationships, and perhaps others, will fall into your area.

For example, an increasing number of retirees are tapping the equity in their homes to increase their cash flow. These "Reverse Equity Mortgages" may come across as counter-intuitive to many clients, whose whole goal has been to pay off the mortgage. However, some retirees who had counted on stock market profits and saw their accounts deflate in the tech bust, have turned to these vehicles to supplement retirement income. In such situations, you as CRO may need to help coordinate relationships with bankers, real estate professionals, and even appraisers.

Coordinate with an Attorney

The main relationship, and one that can be most challenging for your clients, is with a lawyer. No matter how large or small the estate, having something from a simple will to a comprehensive estate plan that ensures your client's property will be protected, wishes will be honored, and loved ones will be provided for.

The importance of a will is obvious. Without a will, the State is left to decide who is entitled to your clients' personal items and who is granted custody of minor children. However, over 70 percent of Americans don't have a will for myriad reasons, including time constraints, fear of high cost, and the requirement to think about their mortality.

What does my CRO do?
Focuses on ME!
Manages risk.
Emphasizes net worth, not income.

Surveys show that men are less comfortable than women when discussing their own eventual death. Most think they are either too young or too fit to talk about it. Married women should be more practical. They tend to live longer than men, and most are younger than their husbands. These two facts together can spell many years of self-reliance for women after years of shared responsibility. In general, married women should plan to be on their own.

For most people, visiting a lawyer is an unusual event that involves stress and cost. The requirements of a will often change as circumstances change: as children become adults, as marriages break up, and as assets change and grow. The younger people are when they prepare a will, the greater the likelihood it will need to be changed later, resulting in fresh legal fees. This is reason enough for many to delay this acknowledgement of mortality.

Most adults understand they should have a will, but most don't expect to die tomorrow. Tomorrow never comes, as the saying goes. But with each new day, tomorrow becomes today. We have no way of knowing which "today" will be our last. Maybe that's why most people die without a will, or why their will is not up-to-date. As a CRO, you should require your clients to sit down with their attorney. If they do not have one, recommend one or several from whose services they can choose.

Prepare is a good acronym for the many things a CRO needs to remember and stay on top of during the process of disbursing clients' retirement funds (See Figure 11.2). Compared to saving for retirement, taking the money out of retirement plans is full of complexities. As CRO, this promises to be an area of increasing importance as clients approach the ages that they want, or must, start receiving payouts. The particulars of your clients' plans will govern what you need to do. Ask open-ended questions to help determine their needs and motives, and then discuss what you recommend, and why.

Plan for your clients to take required minimum distributions. Create a distribution strategy with your clients by asking questions such as: "When do you need the IRA money?" "Who is the beneficiary of your IRA?" "What do you want your IRA to do for you?" Follow this six-step protocol when developing distribution plans:

1. *Review beneficiaries.* Make sure clients name primary and contingent beneficiaries. The designated beneficiaries have the right to disclaim interest from the inherited IRA. They do not have to take advantage of this right, but without a contingent beneficiary listed, it will not be possible to "stretch" the IRA. This is a no-cost strategy that gives ultimate flexibility in the future. This is the first step for implementing the distribution strategy. If the IRA is set up incorrectly, the beneficiary (who may be your future client) may be faced with a tax problem.

2. *Educate yourself on custodian requirements.* All of your planning

FIGURE 11.2	**Prepare for Distributions** **A CRO should P.R.E.P.A.R.E. for distributions**
	Plan for required distributions.
	Review beneficiaries.
	Educate about custodian requirements.
	Partner with an attorney.
	Annually review.
	Rollover to consolidate assets
	Establish separate accounts for beneficiaries

could be for nothing if the custodian or trustee does not allow for certain beneficiaries, does not have a record of the beneficiary, inputs the beneficiary incorrectly, or gets the BDA (beneficiary distribution account) registration incorrect.

3. *Partner with the client's attorney.* Make sure the estate plan works in conjunction with the IRA distribution strategy. Clients should consult with an attorney to implement any estate planning recommendations regarding qualified plans and IRAs. Remember: CROs do not provide tax and/ or legal advice.

4. *Annually review the plan.* It makes sense to sit down with your client at least annually to go over beneficiary designations. Situations change. Was there a divorce or death in the family? Did a child or grandchild join the family? Update the plan's strategies to keep retirement investments in line with goals, time horizon, and risk tolerance.

5. *Consolidate assets in one place with rollovers and transfers.* IRAs offer choices and flexibility that aren't found in employer-sponsored plans like 401(k)s. Consider rolling assets from former employer plans into the IRA. Then bring all the IRAs under one roof. That makes it easier to put an overall stretch strategy into place and will probably save fees too.

6. *Establish separate accounts for beneficiaries.* Upon the death of an IRA owner, multiple beneficiaries have until December 31 of the year following

death to split the inherited IRA into separate accounts using their own life expectancies to calculate distributions. If the IRA is not split, distributions are calculated using the oldest beneficiary's life expectancy. Make certain that the beneficiaries are clear on what has to happen when they inherit IRA assets. Explain to them that you are the contact person at the time of your client's death and have all the necessary documentation.

Your Value as Your Client's CRO

Founding Father, Benjamin Franklin, was known for using a T-graph to weigh both sides of an issue by writing out the pros list on one side and the cons list on the other side of the T. Ahead in Chapter 13, I share a way you can use the Franklin T-graph as a tool with your clients as they ponder their "lump-sum dilemma" and how they'll be able to (financially) make it to 59 1/2, 62, and 100. The key to the Franklin T-graph exercise, though, is to reaffirm to both you, the CRO, and to your clients, that working with you provides an incredible value to help them through their financial retirement situations.

Chapter 12, *The IRA Beneficiary Dilemma*, goes into specific detail on the IRA and beneficiary dilemma. For many of your clients, it really is a big enough deal to deserve its own chapter. Why? Helping your clients decide about beneficiaries and unwind the complexities is a perfect example of the value-added that you as CRO bring to your clients. It gets to the heart of the expertise you can provide your clients. They don't know it, but they need to decide the purpose of their IRA. Will it be needed for current income for a remaining spouse in the case of the IRA owner's death? Or perhaps the spouse has other sources of income. In that case, there are ways of structuring the beneficiaries to leave a legacy for children and/or grandchildren. In your role as CRO, you can help clients see the different ways their IRAs may be tapped—or stretched.

Plow the field to prepare for success. Follow the lead of the doctor and ask questions first, to uncover stories, values, goals, and motives. Use the organizer provided by your firm to collect the key information to do your job effectively. By painting scenarios with your clients and playing "what if" with computer models, you will show your clients that there's more than one way to consider the retirement possibilities. You can explain the reasons behind your recommendations. You're not just trying to sell them something. You need to make sure your clients get that annual financial checkup, work with the rest of their financial team of advisors, and manage risk even in the context of disbursing their assets throughout a long life.

Use the CRO process as outlined in this chapter to affirm your value and build a solid business with your clients. As CRO, you're making a lifetime commitment for and with your clients. I want to wrap up this chapter with my "value of a professional" quiz. Read through the following statement and count the number of "F's" that you see. It's not a trick.

FINISHED FILES ARE THE RESULT OF YEARS OF SCIENTIFIC STUDY COMBINED WITH THE EXPERIENCE OF MANY YEARS.

How many "F's" did you spot?

Here's how the value of a professional shines through. If you're too close to a situation, you may not spot all the "F's" (*By the way, there are six "F's"*). Sometimes our clients are so enmeshed in their own lives that they have trouble putting things in perspective. As financial professionals, we can help.

Chapter 12

THE IRA BENEFICIARY DILEMMA

"These three things are certain. The first two are death and taxes. The third is that, without preparation, a gross amount of the latter will follow the former."
  - *Mitch Anthony, Author*

John and Lynne's IRA Makes Them Unexpected Millionaires

Seventy-year-old John and his wife Lynne, 68, have an estate worth $2 million. The estate consists of a home that has increased in value dramatically over the last ten years, a few investments, some CDs, a bank account, and John's IRA, now worth $1 million.

John and Lynne saved diligently, putting away as much as they could in John's company 401(k). John rolled over his retirement plan distribution to an IRA when he retired. Saving for retirement was a matter of discipline. "If you don't see it, you won't miss it," was their attitude.

Now, however, John observes, "I've been saving for 40 years. Saving was easy compared to the planning required to take it out!" IRA distributions can be a complex task.

A Hobson's Choice

In the late 1500s in Cambridge, England, there was stable manager named Tobias Hobson who rented horses. Like any owner of a large number of horses, he had some good horses and some not-so-good horses. Once the best working horses were rented, people would pass him by to rent from another stable. Tobias

Hobson came up with an idea. He insisted customers take the horse in the stall closest to the door (the next one up) or take none at all. Thus, a Hobson's choice, made famous by the author Milton, has come to mean a choice without an alternative—two options that are equally undesirable. In 1914, Henry Ford offered customers of the Model T a famous Hobson's choice, making it available in "any color so long as it is black."

When planning for IRA distributions, clients sometimes face a Hobson's choice.

John and Lynne do not feel like millionaires, but they are about to run into a millionaire couple's problems. If asked, John and Lynne would say they never thought they would be rich enough for an estate plan. Many of your clients may think the same thing. It could be a costly mistake for your client and for you. These "unconscious millionaires" have seen only the reality of what they can spend. In one sense, they may be right. Given the current climate, income generated by a million dollars over a year's time is about $40,000, hardly what it takes to fund a lavish lifestyle. Even with their million-plus nest egg, John and Lynne are hardly in the same category as the "Gilligan's Island" millionaires, Thurston Howell, III and his wife, Lovey.

IRA and qualified plan distributions are among the most misunderstood areas of retirement and estate planning. IRA tax regulations are complex, and applying them requires planning. With good planning, you can minimize the tax bite. Many married couples face a classic estate planning dilemma. They have combined estates large enough to require them to pay estate taxes, but each spouse has insufficient separate assets—other than retirement plans—to fund a bypass trust that could cut their estate tax bill.

The issue for John and Lynne's CRO is that Lynne is currently listed as the beneficiary of John's IRA account. If John dies, all the property goes to Lynne. Upon Lynne's death, their only child, daughter Jackie, inherits everything. Lynne's estate will owe federal estate tax. Taxes are due within nine months of Lynne's death, payable by Jackie. If Jackie needs to dip into the IRA to pay the taxes, it means more taxes will be due. The problem at this point starts reflecting back at you, the CRO. That's because the person you are explaining this to is Jackie. She may doubt your skills because all she sees is her parents' wealth—what they worked so hard for their whole lives—being given to the taxman instead of their child and grandchildren.

Like John and Lynne, your clients face tradeoffs. There is no one right answer for every situation. Therefore, it's your role as CRO to open this discussion with your clients. There are three primary questions:

1. When do you need the IRA money?

2. Who is the beneficiary of your IRA?

3. What do you want your IRA to do for you?

When Do You Need the IRA Money?

IRAs are designed primarily to provide retirement income but may also provide long-term financial benefits for beneficiaries. Many clients want to continue compounded tax-deferred growth for as long as possible. The IRA must start providing distributions known as required minimum distributions (RMDs) when clients reach age 70 1/2, known as the required beginning date (RBD).

Actually, the first payment can be delayed until April 1 of the year following the year the client turns age 70 1/2. Remember, if IRA owners delay the first payment, they must also take a second RMD by December 31 of the same year. All subsequent RMDs must be taken by December 31 of the year in which it is due. If clients miss the deadline or fail to take out enough, they will pay an additional 50 percent tax on the money that should have come out. The RMD is calculated by taking the previous year's December 31 account balance and dividing by the factor for the client's age found on the IRS's Uniform Lifetime Table. The only exception to the rule is if the spouse is ten or more years younger. Then, a couple may use a more advantageous IRS table, based on actuarial assumptions that if the wife is that much younger, then she is likely to outlive her husband by quite a bit and will need some of the money.

Who Is the Beneficiary of Your IRA?

During the IRA owner's lifetime, the beneficiary does not matter. The required minimum distributions do not depend on the beneficiary. An account owner can change beneficiaries anytime while alive without negatively impacting RMD. However, all designated beneficiaries must be named as of the date of death in order to inherit the IRA assets.

Beneficiaries must be determined by September 30 of the year after the account owner dies. This delay allows primary beneficiaries some strategy time. They must decide several things. Most importantly, this time allows them to decide if they do want and/or need to be the beneficiary. A primary beneficiary may disclaim any or all of the assets in the account. Then the assets move on to the contingent beneficiary, provided one is listed. In order to disclaim the IRA assets, the beneficiary must:

- Put the disclaimer in writing within nine months of death;

- Not have accepted any benefits from the retirement plans or IRA;

- Pass without providing any direction on the part of the disclaiming beneficiary.

Disclaimers can be a useful tool but may involve complications that are beyond the scope of this book, especially when qualified pension plans or trusts are involved. Rules for inheriting an IRA depend on who the beneficiary of your IRA is.

Spousal Beneficiary
Many IRA owners designate their spouses as primary beneficiaries, with good reason. A surviving spouse may need the IRA assets for financial support. Ask the question, "When do you need the money?" There are two options when a spouse inherits an IRA:

1. *The surviving spouse can roll the inherited IRA into his own new or existing IRA.* For a spouse who is younger then 70 1/2, the advantage is that he can delay RMDs until age 70 1/2, which increases the power of tax deferral and compounding. The spouse is also eligible to make annual contributions to the IRA, as long as there is earned income.

2. *The surviving spouse may transfer the inherited IRA to a beneficiary distribution account (BDA).* The distributions are based on the surviving spouse's life expectancy. If the surviving spouse is younger than 59 1/2 and needs to tap into the IRA for funds, creating a beneficiary distribution account (BDA) will allow her to do so without incurring a ten percent early withdrawal penalty.

The designated beneficiary distribution account (BDA) registration should look something like this:

> XYZ Trust Company
> Custodian for the IRA of John Jones, deceased
> For the Benefit of (FBO) Lynne Jones, beneficiary

The BDA account uses the beneficiary's tax identification number for distributions. If your client is the "For the Benefit of" (FBO), she is the owner. The new owner can now direct how the funds are invested, name new primary and contingent beneficiaries, and move the account from one custodian to another.

Non-Spousal Beneficiaries

Non-spousal beneficiaries have two choices on how to take distributions:

1. *Five-Year Rule.* To use the five-year rule, beneficiaries must withdraw all assets from the inherited IRA by December 31 of the fifth year following the IRA owner's death. The five-year rule allows beneficiaries to withdraw assets, at any time, in any amount, as long as the IRA is depleted within the five-year timeframe. Distributions come out penalty-free. Ordinary income taxes are owed. This schedule might work well for clients who need the assets. Large distributions, however, could be a tax burden. Be aware of what is known as the tax bracket creep, as large distributions may put the receiver into a higher tax bracket.

2. *Life Expectancy.* Non-spousal beneficiaries may have the IRA proceeds paid out over their own life expectancies and pay ordinary income taxes on the distributed amounts. To use the life expectancy method, it must be implemented no later than December 31 of the year following the year of the IRA owner's death. If the election is not made by that date, then the five-year rule discussed above kicks in.

The life expectancy method is also known as a "stretch IRA." The stretch IRA is not a different kind of IRA; it is a strategy to use with the traditional IRA. This strategy helps to control and minimize the taxes required on distributions from an IRA.

Daughter Jackie Would be Non-Spousal Beneficiary

John and Lynne's situation works like this: John named Lynne, his spouse, as the beneficiary to his IRA. When John passes away, Lynne names their daughter Jackie as beneficiary and stretches payments over Lynne's life expectancy. When Lynne passes away, Jackie would name a new beneficiary and stretch payments over Jackie's life expectancy.

The stretch IRA maximizes the IRA's tax-deferred growth and helps leave a legacy. However, the stretch IRA may not be suitable for everyone. It is designed for people who have sources of income (other than their IRAs) to fund retirement expenses.

Multiple beneficiaries have until December 31 of the year following death to split the inherited IRA into separate accounts using their own life expectancies to calculate distributions. If the IRA is not split, then distributions are calculated using the oldest beneficiary's life expectancy.

Estate, Trust, or Charitable Beneficiaries

Although the trust can never be the owner of the IRA, an estate, a Q-TIP or Credit Shelter Trust, a charity or any other legal entity can be made an IRA beneficiary. Certain rules must be carefully followed to make a trust a "qualified trust" meeting IRS guidelines. Basically, to establish a trust as the beneficiary of an IRA, the trust must:

1. Be valid under state law.

2. Be irrevocable, or a revocable trust that becomes irrevocable upon the date of death.

3. Have identifiable beneficiaries of the trust.

4. Provide a copy of the trust to the custodian or trustee of the IRA (Often, the first and last pages of the trust are provided to the custodian or trustee).

The trust beneficiaries must be easily identified and must be individuals. To compute the minimum required distributions to the trust, the life expectancy of the oldest beneficiary is used as the measuring life.

If these rules are not met, then the benefits will still bypass the surviving spouse's estate, but the five-year rule will apply if the participant dies before the RBD. If the participant dies after the RBD, distributions are made to the trust from the life expectancy tables.

Estate Tax Issues

The reason all this is important is that upon the death of the retirement plan owner, the federal government levies an estate tax. The estate tax is on the wealth of the deceased. Some states impose an estate tax beyond the federal tax, while other states take part of the federal estate tax. Retirement funds are a part of the taxable estate. The Economic Growth and Tax Relief Reconciliation Act of 2001 (EGTRRA) repealed the estate tax over a ten-year period. The estate tax will go to zero percent in 2010 under this law. However, the estate tax comes back in 2011 unless changed by future legislation. Therefore, the perfect time for your client to die is in 2010! Since there are many unknown variables, we can only plan from today to 2010.

In 2004, each person has a $1.5 million exemption from the tax. Thus, husband and wife get $1.5 million each. However, if clients leave everything to their spouses, they lose the $1.5 million deduction.

Under current tax law, you can leave as much as you want to your spouse estate tax-free. This is called the unlimited marital deduction. The government levies no tax until the surviving spouse's death. The unlimited marital deduction causes many couples to lose the estate tax deduction when the first spouse dies. Your client can only use the exemption when the estate is left to someone other than the spouse.

While naming a trust as beneficiary uses a couple's unified credits, it generally results in some disadvantages. Since retirement and IRA benefits are considered "income in respect of a decedent" (IRD), they are generally included in gross income upon receipt. IRD paid to a trust is typically taxed at higher rates than IRD paid to an individual.

What Do You Want Your IRA to Do for You?

Back to John and Lynne

Lynne is the beneficiary of John's account. If John dies, everything goes to Lynne: all the property (totaling $1 million) and the IRA (also $1 million). John lost his estate tax deduction. Upon Lynne's death, their daughter Jackie inherits the property and the IRA. Lynne's estate owes federal estate tax. Taxes are due within nine months of Lynne's death, payable by Jackie. If Jackie needs to dip into the IRA to pay the taxes, more taxes are due.

However, Lynne and Jackie could both stretch the IRA, thereby minimizing income taxes. This option minimizes income taxes at the expense of potentially higher estate taxes.

As a second option, John names daughter Jackie as the beneficiary of the IRA. When John dies, all the property goes to Lynne, reducing the value of John's estate to zero. Jackie gets the IRA and stretches over her life expectancy. Upon Lynne's death, their daughter Jackie inherits everything. Lynne gets the estate tax exemption. No federal estate tax is due. This is the most efficient tax alternative. In this case, the clients are minimizing the income tax by stretching the IRA and also minimizing estate taxes since the IRA benefits are removed from Lynne's estate. The problem is Lynne loses control of the IRA during her life and gives up half of the inheritance. Many clients prefer that the surviving spouse has access to the IRA assets if needed.

A third option is to name a qualified bypass trust as the IRA beneficiary. Retirement benefits can bypass the surviving spouse's estate. Even though the benefits are paid to a trust, Lynne can still use the income and principal generated by the trust assets, if needed. However, the trust probably will pay higher income taxes on the benefits than either Lynne or Jackie would. Moreover, the stretch opportunities for Lynne or Jackie are forfeited.

A fourth option is to name Lynne as the primary beneficiary and Jackie as contingent beneficiary of the IRA. If Lynne does not need the IRA assets, she disclaims upon John's death. They then pass on the assets to Jackie who can stretch. This option lets the CRO and Lynne take a second look at estate assets after the death of the first spouse. If John had named a bypass trust as contingent beneficiary in the event of a disclaimer, this would achieve the same benefits.

CROs Can Help Clarify Clients' IRA Options

So John and Lynne have options and tradeoffs to make. As their CRO, you need to know the answers to "What do you want your IRA to do for you?" and "When do you need the money?" Only then will you be able to help clients answer, "Who *should* be the beneficiary to your IRA?"

IRA distributions offer great planning opportunities for a family's CRO. However, no general rule will fit every situation. The plan must fit each client's specific needs. The choices appear straightforward in our neat and tidy example of a married couple, both conveniently dying before RBD, with one child. That's not how real life works. Second marriages, multiple children, stepchildren, grandchildren, disinherited children, and favorite nephews: all these commonplace issues increase the complexities of beneficiary planning. As CRO, you must know a great deal about your clients.

The discussion here touched on only some of the basic issues. Each of the alternatives is appropriate for different cases. You must take into account the facts and circumstances involved in each client's particular situation. You should prepare clients so they can give careful thought to whom they name as a beneficiary of their IRA or retirement plan. In the context of their preferred recipient, the answers may be simple. As we've seen in this story, putting in the correct strategy may not be so easy.

Couples like John and Lynne have an image of millionaires in their heads, and the image doesn't match the reality of who they are. They may subconsciously feel that millionaires are more like Thurston Howell, III and Lovey on the TV show *Gilligan's Island*. The Howells maintained an attitude of privilege and entitlement, even after being shipwrecked on a deserted island with a hand full of regular, less financially well-endowed folks. Yet, John and Lynne, the regular folks—the unconscious millionaires—now have to step up to decision-making on IRA beneficiaries with similar Howell-like confidence.

Chapter 13

HOW WILL YOUR CLIENTS MAKE IT TO 59 ½, 62, & 100?

"Birthdays are good for you; the more you have, the longer you live."
 - Unknown

Jim Hilker's Early Retirement Leads Him to Ask,
"How Will We Make It to 59 1/2, 62 and then 100?"

Jim Hilker looks like any other retiree, clad in khaki shorts and golf shirt, plotting his next fix-it project on the patio of his stucco home. But the 58-year-old has gone back to work for less than his salary was four years ago, when he took an early-retirement package from his job maintaining equipment for the phone company.

Back then, his retirement seemed secure and comfortable, with a fat nest egg. Now, his savings have plummeted due to the lagging stock market. Right now, his concern is that he can't stop the money from coming. He locked himself into an annuity payout. Leery of losing more in the market, he uses part of the money for living and plunks the rest into a savings account. "I'm not broke, but I still have to work," Mr. Hilker muses, saying it was a "mistake" to agree to a mandatory-withdrawal plan. "I just wish I had taken the option to spread it over my lifetime as well as that of my spouse."

"We could probably make it without the paycheck," Mr. Hilker says. "But I don't want to have something happen to us and have my kids worry about where we're going to get the money to pay for it."

And what about retirement? Mr. Hilker had thought about giving it a second try at age 60, when he will start collecting his military pension. But given the turmoil in the stock markets, he says he might wait until 62, when he can collect Social Security.

It could be a difficult journey. Mr. Hilker recently received a letter from his former company saying that his quarterly premium for health insurance, one of his best retirement benefits, was being raised to $400 from $150. "With everything going on right now," he says, "I'm just glad I've got a job."

Like Jim Hilker, an increasing number of people will work in retirement, whether they will need the money or just want the mental stimulation and interactions with people. Those, like Mr. Hilker, in an early retirement situation, are even more likely to work. Often working without benefits or retirement plans, these early retirees may take a "bridge job," to bridge their main career with their ultimate retirement. For many others, the opportunity to be their own boss means they will consult in their field or start their own small business, often based on a long-time interest or hobby.

Three Financial Milestones

As CRO, you can help all these people meet three key milestones: accessing retirement accounts without penalty (generally 59 1/2); receiving Social Security (a sliding scale from ages 62 to 67, depending on their birth year and whether they choose full or reduced benefits); and helping their money last for their increasing life spans (with living to 100 a real possibility for many).

The accumulated wealth of the Baby Boom generation will be heavily concentrated in employer-sponsored retirement plans and IRAs. The concepts for these tax-deferred vehicles have been pretty simple up to this point: contribute and take full advantage of the plan. To date, the value-added for the financial services industry has been on the asset allocation side of the business. As the Baby Boom Generation heads to the first transition in retirement, a whole new bevy of issues will crop up. The value-added of the financial services industry will be the ability to understand the needs of clients and to guide them through the maze of procedures so that they can access their retirement money.

Clients will need your help developing a payout strategy for the income phase of retirement—and doing it in such a way that the money will last to meet their needs, including an ever-increasing percentage devoted to health costs.

Opening the Conversation: "How Will I Make it to 59 1/2, 62, and 100?"

Let's say your clients are 56-years-old. They are sitting in your office freaking out. They ask, "How are we going to make it to 59 1/2, 62, and 100?" At age 59 1/2, they can access their retirement plan assets without a penalty, and this will represent the largest portion of their wealth. Clients can start collecting Social Security at age 62. And, the fastest-growing age group in America today are those over 100 years old. This means one thing: eventually Willard Scott will be wishing happy birthday to people for the entire show. It will be like the happy birthday show.

Let me ask you: can you help couples like the Hilkers with the "Will I make it…?" question? Don't you have access to retirement planning calculators? Doesn't the computer on your desk give you access to all the different ways to find the answer to your clients' question, "How do I make it to 59 1/2, 62, and 100?"

If your clients aren't concerned, maybe you should prod them. "You may be worried about how you are going to make it to 59 1/2, 62, and 100." Recap for clients what these milestones mean, then continue, "A lot of my clients are concerned. Well, let me reassure you that I have all the resources of my firm here at my fingertips to figure this out. And guess what? There is no right or wrong way. What you need to do is tell me what you would like your retirement to look like, and I'll plot a course to get there. Then, we will review it on a regular basis because things change."

Here's a question you might use to open the "How will you make it…?" conversation. "Have you ever thought about how much *less stress* you would have in your life if you knew you were on track toward achieving your financial goals?" Because many people may be in a stressful situation at any given time anyway—especially if they are in the midst of a downsizing event—this is another key opportunity to provide value-added as their CRO.

Distributions Options from Retirement Plans

First, we will concentrate on lump sum distribution options from qualified retirement plans. This first step acknowledges that many people will be downsized, select (or be selected for) early retirement, or otherwise leave a full-time job with an organization that offered some kind of retirement plan. Earlier we talked about the stressful decision-making process and how leaving a workplace is a stressful event for most clients and prospects. The lump sum distribution dilemma, for many, recognizes that one way to reduce stress is to reduce the number of decisions. Your clients may think it's less stressful to do nothing, to make no decision about their retirement plan money from the company they just left. Your goal as CRO is to help them through the stress to see that when they take more control over their financial future, they will actually experience less stress.

A lump sum distribution from an employer's qualified retirement plan occurs when a distribution of the participant's vested account balance is made within one calendar year. Distributions can be made for several reasons: death, disability (except for the self-employed), separation from service (except for the self-employed), and attainment of retirement age.

A plan participant has several options upon terminating from service: the decisions regarding what to do with the retirement plan assets after termination from the plan are really quite simple. Yet if your clients have to make the decision at one of the most stressful times of their lives, it is easy to do so incorrectly. Often, as Jim Hilker discovered, these early decisions are irrevocable. As CRO, your mission is to help your clients make the best decisions for their situations the first time. There are three basic choices:

1. *Cash in the distribution.* The employer is required to withhold 20 percent of the distribution and send it to the IRS as prepayment of income taxes owed on the distribution. Participants may not owe this much. The difference is refunded when taxes are filed for the year. Current income tax is owed on the distribution amount and, if the client is younger than 59 1/2, a ten percent penalty is added on.

   Taxes can be paid three different ways:

   • *Pay the taxes owed based on current income tax bracket.*

   • *Use ten-year averaging method.*

   • *Take a lump sum distribution and net unrealized appreciation.*

2. *Leave it with the old employer's plan or move it to the new employer's plan.* If a participant has an account balance greater than $5,000, the plan cannot force former employees to leave unless they are terminating the plan. In order to move it to the new employer's plan, the new employer's plan must allow for rollovers.

3. *Roll to an IRA*. A **direct rollover** results in no withholding, no penalty, and no income tax paid. The money is moved directly from the account in the employer's plan into the employee's account as an IRA custodian.

With an **indirect rollover**, the employer is required to withhold 20 percent of the distribution and send it to the IRS as prepayment of income taxes on the distribution. The participant has 60 days to roll over 100 percent of the distribution to avoid penalties and taxes, which includes the amount withheld by the employer. If the participant is unable to come up with the 20 percent withheld, the amount not rolled over (with the 20 percent withheld) will be taxed at the current income tax rate; plus, if under age 59 1/2, an additional ten-percent penalty will be added onto the amount not rolled over.

Those are basically your clients' options. Once your clients decide on the option, then they have other decisions to make.

What do most job changers do with the money after changing jobs? Cerulli Associates did a study on job changers and how they handled their distributions. Here are their findings:

- 18% cashed in their distribution
- 12% kept it in the old employer's plan
- 3% moved it to the new plan
- 67% rolled to an IRA[1]

As CRO, your two prospecting opportunities are the people who leave their retirement funds in the old plan and those who move to an IRA. The majority of workers make IRA rollovers.

Using the Franklin T-Graph to Illustrate the CRO's Value in a Rollover

I conduct a lot of workshops with financial professionals. One exercise that helps them highlight the value of their services is the Ben Franklin Decision T-graph, which is basically a compare/contrast chart for evaluating two choices prior to making a decision.

Many advisors come across people who leave their money in the plan, unable to move. Your goal is to put the value of your services in context for your prospects. When prospects see the completed T-graph analysis, they should conclude, "It's a no-brainer when you think about it like that." Using the Franklin T-graph is an interactive way to help your clients or prospects evaluate the "return on investment" of working with you. It will help them justify spending money on your service and visualize the resulting value of the purchase or investment, in this case, rolling over their retirement fund to an IRA with you as their CRO.

DIRECTIONS

1. See Figure 13.1.
2. Ask the clients to list as many reasons as they can for why to "Leave in Plan."
3. Do the same for "Roll to an IRA."
4. Ask questions about each feature and prioritize.

FIGURE 13.1

Franklin T-Graph

Leave in Plan	Roll to IRA

Using the Graph with Clients

I've also done the Franklin T-graph in front of actual clients, and their top three answers are: easy, investments, and fees (See Figure 13.2).

1. *It's Easy.* Or as I like to say, "In a stressful decision-making model, when there are a lot of decisions to make, if there is one decision you can make which obviates having to make more decisions, that's a decision you'll make: the decision to not make decisions." However, "it's easy" means multiple things: "no paperwork," "no hassles," "nothing to do," and "leaves me with flexibility."

2. *The Investments.* How many CROs have heard this one? "I like the investments." You say, "Really. What are you invested in?" They say, "It's a 401(k)." You respond, seeking clarification, "No, I understand it's a 401(k). What's the underlying investment?" They say, "It's a 401(k)," a little slower and louder like you suddenly don't speak English.

3. *Fees.* The discussion of fees is really a discussion of value. Price is an issue only in the absence of value. In my workshops, this is the point I move to "Roll to an IRA." This is where you as CRO can present the value-added that your services bring to clients. Before we do, we need to acknowledge that there are some strategic advantages (for certain people in some situations) to leaving retirement money in the company plan.

FIGURE 13.2	Franklin T-Graph—What Clients Say
Leave in Plan	**Roll to IRA**
Easy Investments Fees	

Advantages to Leaving Retirement Money in the Plan

Federal Creditor Protection. An IRA is NOT protected against bankruptcy, malpractice, divorce, lawsuits, and any other bids on clients' assets. Many states provide creditor protection for the IRA, but the federal government does not. The employer plan is ruled under federal legislation, and so clients' funds are protected, except in cases of divorce.

Loans. Clients cannot borrow from their IRAs. Some people may be able to borrow from an employer's retirement plan. Not all employers allow for loans. For those who have terminated service with the employer, it is important to check loan eligibility.

Life Insurance. Money in a qualified plan can be used to buy life insurance. IRA money cannot buy life insurance. If clients have trouble qualifying for life insurance, this may be the only option. If clients are thinking of leaving the plan, but this is the only place they can get life insurance, advise that they think twice about this decision.

Delayed RMD. Those still working at age 70 1/2 do not have to take required minimum distributions. The "still working" exception does not apply to IRAs. It also does not apply to those who are five percent owners of a company.

Age 55 and Up. If clients are at least 55-years-old and leave their jobs, they can get distributions from the retirement plan directly and avoid the ten percent penalty for under age 59 1/2 distributions. Income tax is still owed.

Illustrating Your Value

You must control clients' perception of your value. Many times clients do not see a difference between what you provide and what they can do by themselves. Especially for clients who don't have a lot of experience working with financial professionals, when you say "service," they don't always have a concrete idea of what you can do for them. Maybe they're wondering, "So, do you take care of my car's checkups?!"

You must create a value gap between what you bring to a client in terms of who you are and what you provide (See the "CROs A.R.E." sidebar) versus what clients can do for themselves.

Remember when we talked about workplace and retirement changes as if they were raft trips down a whitewater river? Few people would choose to make the trip without an experienced river guide. They are willing to pay to have the guide along. As CRO, you're their guide through the whitewater of changing retirements.

> *CROs' A.R.E. ...*
> *Attention that you pay to your clients and their needs.*
> *Resources and skills that you bring to the table and/or have access to in your firm or through other strategic professional alliances.*
> *Expertise and technical knowledge about financial and lifestyle issues in retirement.*

Roll to an IRA

Let's now cover what a CRO does on the other side of the T-graph. As illustrated in Figure 13.3, here are some of the reasons for rolling to an IRA, all of which are opportunities for you as CRO to add value.

The Advantages of Rolling to an IRA

Flexibility and Control: IRAs provide more flexibility than a retirement plan. If clients need to get the money from an IRA, they can, even if they are younger than 59 1/2. With 401(k) plans, clients need to qualify for the hardship withdrawals. With an IRA, no permission is necessary. The client is in complete control.

Portability: An IRA can move back into a plan.

FIGURE 13.3	Franklin T-Graph—Why Roll to an IRA?
Leave in Plan	**Roll to IRA**
Easy	Control
Investments	Consolidation
Fees	Beneficiaries Options
	Investments
	Advice

Consolidation: Save on fees and on statements (convenience).

Stretch IRA: The beneficiaries can stretch the IRA over their life expectancy. Although distribution would be required, they can stretch over the life expectancy of the beneficiary. That allows the beneficiary to control the taxation and allows the IRA to continued to grow tax deferred. A non-spouse beneficiary in a 401(k) cannot roll to an IRA. The account usually is paid out in a lump sum or over a five-year period, which can lead to a tax problem.

Investment Choices: The IRA has a universe of investment choices to pick from plus the ability to customize investment choices to meet personal needs. A 401(k) may have good options but will be limited and designed for the largest audience possible.

Roth: The option to convert to a Roth is possible only if the account is in an IRA. The Roth conversion allows the account owner to prepay taxes for the beneficiaries. A Roth IRA has no mandatory withdrawals. Conversions to a Roth can never come directly from a retirement plan.

Estate Planning: You can name any primary and contingent beneficiaries, even split accounts. Retirement plans are covered under federal law, and so if clients want to name someone other than the spouse, they must obtain a waiver.

Making it to 62…or 67: Accessing Social Security

Jim Hilker can start to receive his military pension at age 60. At 62, workers can tap into their Social Security. Most people will likely choose to take their Social Security as early as they can, even if it means a smaller amount, on the assumption that a check in hand is better than one never received due to one's untimely passing. Others argue that, since Baby Boomers are reshaping retirement—just as they've reshaped every other stage they've passed through—they may tend not to make the assumed choices.

Most of your clients and prospects are likely to see Social Security as a little extra for their safety net, as icing on the cake rather than the main course. All the media attention leaves no one with the illusion that Social Security is going to be a big retirement bonanza.

On the other hand, for all its problems, Social Security is unlikely to completely disappear. However, the rules will change, and payout times may be extended even more. As CRO, you'll stay on top of the rule changes to help keep your clients informed.

You and your clients can check out the *www.ssa.gov* site for detailed information on Social Security, benefits, and even calculators. Figure 13.4 details the percentage of benefit reductions for accessing Social Security checks before "full retirement age." Figure 13.5 shows the exact "full retirement age," which is based on birth year. Many people still think "65." Most in the Baby Boom generation will have to wait a bit longer than 65 if they go for the "full retirement payout."

Adding Value by Helping Clients Fund the Life They Choose to Live

Your clients will have many productive years during what we now call "retirement." In fact, their increasing life spans mean that many people have a good chance of becoming centenarians. Listening to your clients means you can uncover their hidden dreams, passions, and life purposes. This is the time that they can use their financial resources to address those big dreams—and you can help. In fact, your technical knowledge, skills, expertise, and concern for the well-being of your clients will provide significant added-value in the client relationship to achieve their big picture goals.

According to a report from William L. Anthes and Bruce W. Most, "Retirement in the 21st Century," one of the definitions that best captures the pre-retirees' vision right now is the following: "Retirement is a point in life when a person switches the main focus from economic productivity—earning a living—to self-realization, chasing one's personal goals and aspirations."[2]

FIGURE 13.4	**Benefit Percentages for "Early Access"**[3]

If your full retirement age is older than 65 (that is, you were born after 1937), you still will be able to take your benefits at age 62, but the reduction in your benefit amount will be greater than it is for people retiring now.

Here's how it works. If your full retirement age is 67, then the reduction for starting your retirement benefits at age 62 is about 30 percent. The reduction for starting benefits at age...

- 63 is about 25 percent
- 64 is about 20 percent
- 65 is about 13.3 percent
- 66 is about 6.7 percent

This information comes from http://www.ssa.gov

FIGURE 13.5	**Age To Receive Full Social Security Benefits**[4] (Called "full retirement age" or "normal retirement age")

Year of Birth*	Full Retirement Age
1937 or earlier	65
1938	65 and 2 months
1939	65 and 4 months
1940	65 and 6 months
1941	65 and 8 months
1942	65 and 10 months
1943—1954	66
1955	66 and 2 months
1956	66 and 4 months
1957	66 and 6 months
1958	66 and 8 months
1959	66 and 10 months
1960 and later	67

*If you were born on January 1st of any year you should refer to the previous year. The earliest you can start receiving Social Security retirement benefits will remain age 62.

This information comes from http://www.ssa.gov

Or, to quote Mitch Anthony from *The New Retirementality*, "When people today talk of retiring, they are rarely speaking of retired living; they are usually speaking of emancipated living. They want to be free to pursue their goals, at their pace, and free to find a sense of balance…The New Retirementality requires a shift both in how we plan our lives and how we manage our resources. The work we must do is part philosophical and part fiscal."[5]

Making It to 100

Increased longevity is only fun if you're able to enjoy it! Of course, the waves of Baby Boomers washing up onto the shores of retirement are arguably among the healthiest generation to date. Still, as Jim Hilker is discovering, health (and taking care of downside risks through insurance) comes with a price. And the price tag is rising all the time.

The retirees of tomorrow are going to have to deal with rising health costs. In some cases, this will mean the loss of health benefits they thought they had (as employers increasingly cut legacy costs); long-term care for themselves and increasingly for an aging parent; and stretching out their retirement funds over a lifetime.

Health Benefits and Medicare

As Jim Hilker discovered, health insurance costs are rising. Jim is lucky that his former employer still provides some level of health insurance, albeit at a higher price. Statistics indicate that an increasing share of retirees' financial resources must be earmarked for health care and health insurance. Most retirees recognize that keeping their health is the key to a successful retirement, although few yet recognize the estimated cost of ensuring that. Many of the life-saving advances in medical technology are expensive.

As CRO, part of the story you have to tell clients will focus on the increasing percentage of their retirement assets that will be devoted to covering medical and health care costs. There aren't easy answers, especially as companies steadily decline to carry health insurance for their retirees due to rising prices. All kinds of plans from many sources, both for-profit and not-for-profit, are floating around to address the health care affordability question.

For those who make it to age 65, many people without other resources will qualify for Medicare (See Figure 13.6, excerpted from *www.medicare.gov*).

Long-Term Care

Long-term care insurance is one piece of the retirement puzzle that is becoming increasingly important with the aging of the Boomers. This kind of insurance protects against increased costs of living expenses in later life, when special care may be needed. The price of getting extended care for a disability can be much higher than the risks most of us commonly insure against—that is, protecting homes and autos.

Your clients and prospects are spending years building a nest egg, and a lot of money protecting it, with liability policies like homeowners and automobile insurance. There is another type of asset protection, long-term care (LTC) insurance. Many will need the coverage, even as prices continue to rise.

Long-term care insurance is sometimes part of a benefit package for executives. These are people with substantial assets, and long-term care insurance protects those assets. According to information at Aon.com, "There's now a 50 percent chance that an executive will eventually need extended care. By comparison, chances of a homeowner's claim are only 1 in 88 and just 1 in 47 for an auto accident claim...the annual cost of assisted living with minimal care is $26,000, on average."[7]

For your clients and prospects, whether they're in the corner office or not, such extended medical care effectively eats up their retirement assets as well. It is useful to discuss these concepts with your clients, to help them see the need to protect against this risk.

> *"If current patterns continue, there will be an annual shortfall of at least $45 billion by 2030 between the amount retired Americans need to cover basic expenses and what they have. A new study by the Employee Benefit Research Institute in collaboration with the Milbank Memorial Fund suggests that while many middle-income Americans could provide for their own future by saving 5 percent of compensation annually in addition to the retirement benefits they are already expected to receive, this remedy won't work for many in the lower income brackets."[6]*
>
> *—Results of the study published in the November 2003 EBRI Issue Brief.*

> *"Long-term care isn't just for seniors anymore. Odds are, two in five people will need long-term care before they reach age 65."[8]*
>
> *—from Aon.com*

Spreading Income from Assets Over a Lifetime

Typically financial professionals advise even those in retirement to keep some

FIGURE 13.6	What Is Medicare?

Medicare is a Health Insurance Program for:
- People 65 years of age and older
- Some people with disabilities under age 65
- People with End-Stage Renal Disease (permanent kidney failure requiring dialysis or a transplant)

Generally, you are eligible for Medicare if you or your spouse worked for at least ten years in Medicare-covered employment and you are 65-years-old and a citizen or permanent resident of the United States.

Medicare has Two Parts:

Hospital insurance or Medicare Part A
- Most people do not have to pay for Part A.
- It helps pay for care in a hospital or skilled nursing facility, as well as home health care and hospice care.

Medical insurance or Medicare Part B
- Most people pay monthly for Part B.
- It helps pay for doctors, outpatient hospital care, and other medical services.

Part A (Hospital Insurance)

Helps Pay for:

Care in hospitals as an inpatient, critical access hospitals (small facilities that give limited outpatient and inpatient services to people in rural areas), skilled nursing facilities, hospice care, and some home health care. Information about your coverage under Medicare Part A can be found in the Your Medicare Coverage database.

Cost:

Most people get Part A automatically when they turn age 65. They do not have to pay a monthly payment called a premium for Part A because they or a spouse paid Medicare taxes while they were working.

FIGURE 13.6 continued	What Is Medicare?[9]

Here are some simple guidelines.

You can get Part A at age 65 without having to pay premiums if:

- You are already receiving retirement benefits from Social Security or the Railroad Retirement Board.
- You are eligible to receive Social Scourity or Railroad benefits but have not yet filed for them.
- You or your spouse had Medicare-covered government employment.

Part B (Medical Insurance)

Helps Pay For:

Doctors' services, outpatient hospital care, and some other medical services that Part A does not cover, such as the services of physical and occupational therapists and some home health care. Part B helps pay for these covered services and supplies when they are medically necessary. Information about your coverage under Medicare Part B can be found in the Your Medicare Coverage database.

Cost:

You pay the Medicare Part B premium of $66.60 per month in 2004. This amount may change.

Enrolling in Part B is your choice. You can sign up for Part B anytime during a 7-month period that begins 3 months before you turn 65. If you choose to have Part B, the premium is usually taken out of your monthly Social Security, Railroad Retirement, or Civil Service Retirement payment.

You may have choices in how you get your health care including the Original Medicare Plan, Medicare Managed Care Plans (like HMOs), and Medicare Private Fee-for-Service Plans.

http://www.medicare.gov/

growth in their portfolios, in part to hedge against the return of inflation as well as to ensure that retirees don't run out of money before they run out of life.

Annuities have a negative image in the minds of some clients and financial professionals. That said, a new breed of products are becoming available that meet the specific needs of the large number of retirees who will need some degree of ongoing income, especially as fewer workers will have pensions or other defined benefit plans available as a safety net.

> ### Healthy, Wealthy, and Wise
>
> *As they age, more Boomers fear deteriorating health than financial insecurity*
> - *82% Deteriorating physical health*
> - *66% Not having enough money*
> - *51% Loss of spouse/partner*
> - *26% Not being able to engage in meaningful opportunities*[10]

Others point to annuities' favorable tax treatment. In fact, with all the talk about deferring income to retirement in the accumulation phase, many clients may be startled to learn just how much will be taxed. Dave Blackmon, in an article in the March 2003 *Senior Market Advisor* entitled, "Don't Throw Around Retirement Income," makes a detailed case for using annuities to help clients lower the tax bite in retirement. Knowing the tax implications of your clients' retirement income can have a profound impact on their available assets.[11]

The new products becoming available include a mix of growth, income, and immediate and deferred annuitization. Annuitized assets can provide a lifelong income. Donald Jay Korn points directly to future CROs in a recent *Financial Planning* article, "Not Your Mother's Retirement Products." He says, "Soon-to-be-retired Baby Boomers face extended life expectancies as well as curtailed investment expectations, and many will turn to planners for help."[12]

Mike Henkel, president of Ibbotson Associates, is quoted in Korn's article. "Even with supposedly safe withdrawal rates, investors may still run out of money later on in their lives. If you overlay annuities for part of the portfolio, their prospects look much better."[13] Your goal is to help clients get to 100 with the resources to see them through. If these new products can do the trick, then it's well worth consideration.

Finding out about these hybrid products is just one piece of the ongoing professional education puzzle that you, as CRO, will be responsible for maintaining (See Chapter 15, *Continuing Your Education as CRO* for more). As with long-term care insurance, you may be recommending products for which you receive compensation. The key to success as CRO is first to discuss your clients' needs, then review your process for helping them meet those needs. You can outline alternative ways of getting to the same place. Some choices may be more effective than others in meeting their needs. This way, you can make sure they can see any product recommendations in light of specifically what they are trying to accomplish.

CROs Help Clients Meet Financial Milestones

In addition to providing support for life planning, most CROs have at their disposal a full array of financial products that can help clients streamline their financial pictures. Many financial services firms now offer whole packages of services that can make life easier for clients and meet nearly all their financial needs including mortgages, check-writing and bill payment, credit and ATM cards, and direct deposit. Brokerage firms offer clients a full range of investment products including stocks, bonds, mutual funds, CDs, insurance, and annuities. There are services such as advice on retirement planning, asset allocation, portfolio management, college funding, estate planning, and trust services.

Best of all, they get you—a live person, face-to-face interaction, and someone who knows their story. As a CRO, you are building relationships to help your clients see and deal with the whole of their lives, giving them the tools to make financial decisions so that their retirement assets can support the big picture they envision. They have a lifetime of choices before them and many ways to "make it" to 59 1/2, 62, and 100. As CRO, you can show them their options and ways of expanding their opportunities and choices, even as you're building your own book of business.

Chapter 14

GROWING YOUR RETIREMENT BUSINESS

"Knowing when to keep your mouth shut is invariably more important than opening it at the right time."
 - Malcolm Forbes (1919-1990)

In the process of putting together this book, I have had the opportunity to meet and speak in front of thousands of financial professionals. I've listened to their questions, heard their woes, and shared their success stories. Listening to some of the top-producing financial advisors at firms of all kinds, I've learned the tactics these top producers use to succeed. I want to share some of these ideas with you. They may seem almost simplistic. In fact, in my talks, I tend to call them a "half-dozen dumb ideas" (The publisher wasn't fond of that as a chapter title). These are the ideas and tasks we all know how to do—and know we should do—yet few really have the structures in place to take these simple, daily actions that automatically grow their business.

Every financial professional who masters—and practices—these basics day in and day out will likely have a thriving practice. Too many, though, bypass the basics for new "flavor of the month" sales or marketing approaches, a constantly changing kaleidoscope. From my experience and observations, if you can really take daily actions that encompass these very basic sales and marketing activities, you will experience uncommon success. Everyone *knows* the basics. The key is *doing* them—every single day in a planned and consistent way. We'll look at activities appropriate for building your book of business with both clients and prospects, business-building strategies geared to current clients, and ways to grow your prospecting pipeline.

Business-Building Ideas Appropriate for Both Clients and Prospects

Whether they're already clients and you want to do more business with them, or they are the ideal prospects that perfectly fit your chosen niche, practice these basics to increase your results.

1. Ask Questions—Then Be Quiet and Listen

In an industry where gregarious, outgoing sales types congregate, there's a real tendency to "sell." You just keep talking at clients and prospects—at least that's the stereotype. Listening to what clients and prospects have to say is much more effective. The key is to train yourself to ask open-ended questions that elicit clients' underlying concerns, goals, and priorities.

When selling, effective listening is the difference between success and failure. All successful salespeople are good listeners. That is how they determine the pulse of the buyer, uncover emotional needs, and identify the wants of the buyer. People buy from people they like, people they feel understand them, and people they trust.

To keep uncovering deeper client concerns, ask, "Why?" This is the ultimate open-ended question. Alternatively, you might phrase it as, "Tell me more about that..."

2. Use "StorySelling"

StorySelling, developed by Scott West and Mitch Anthony, is a simple two-step process that uses conversation and open-ended questions to "mine" the clients' lives for individual stories. The StorySelling process relies on a creative thought process that ties the product or service an advisor is selling to the client's known and accepted base of knowledge and experiences. Using StorySelling will help your clients view you not just as an investment representative, but as a consultant who takes the time to illuminate investment concepts that once seemed confusing to them.

During the first step in the StorySelling process, your conversations and open-ended questions with your client will help uncover stories. You'll be like a biographer, mining the client's life, work, and family for individual stories. In this process, you'll uncover both positive and negative experiences that can hurt or help you in the client sales and consulting process. You'll uncover their "goldmines" and get advance warnings about potential "land mines."

Once you begin to understand the client's story, you'll be able to introduce appropriate illustrations and analogies that will resonate with the client's experiences. These stories are simple, yet effective vehicles to communicate complex investment strategies and products in a way your client can understand and relate to.

Successful StorySelling depends on your ability to listen to a client. You ask the probing questions; then, sit back and listen. You will hear their stories and what's important in your client's life. Your job is to use familiar stories to explain something unfamiliar.[1]

Here's an example: You've learned that your 50+-year-old clients Jim and Joan have two children who are in college. You might ask, "Did your children ever go through a year when they went through a real growth spurt—where they really shot up during that year? Well, that's what your growth fund managers are looking for—companies on the verge of that growth spurt. They want to invest in a company that's five feet four and growing—not the company that's already six feet two."

3. Win Business by Educating Clients and Prospects

Another way to win business is to educate them! That may seem counterintuitive. "Why," you might ask, "would I want to educate my clients and prospects when I am the one who needs the knowledge? After all, it's me they come to for their financial planning needs!" On the one hand, nothing could be more correct—you are the expert. On the other hand, numerous surveys and studies have revealed that clients come to financial experts for advice, planning, and education. So, continuing to teach your clients tells them you still care.

One of the best, most cost-effective ways to educate clients is to host large client-retention seminars with a guest speaker on an educational topic of interest. Many times this will be of a financial planning nature; however, it might also include subjects like health care and safety, women's issues, or issues of interest to clients with children.

Similarly, offering an educational seminar, especially as you are prospecting in your ideal niche of potential rollover IRA clients, is again a targeted and efficient way to present your services to a group of people who need help. I mentioned earlier the possibilities of offering seminars through companies that are downsizing, or through the outplacement firms they've hired to help former employees. This is especially effective when it's what I call a "horizontal" downsizing—where everyone at a certain level or particular department is being let go. Recruiters or headhunters are another group of professionals for whom your educational seminars can offer added value to their existing package of services.

4. Use the Branding At Hand

While you are building the one-on-one relationships with your clients and prospects, as CRO you also have ready access to an array of marketing tools and research provided by your firm. Your firm creates mountains of support materials to help you do your job, giving you access to information that is also some of the best and most comprehensive branding available. Use this information to extend your reach with prospects while providing clients with valuable information.

Ways to Build Your Business with Current Clients

The people already in your book of business are the "goldmine" that you want to cultivate. Your goal as CRO is to help them manage all their retirement assets. The first thing you have to avoid is what I call the "*Idintnoyadiddat* Syndrome*.*" Say what?

If a client says to you, "Gee, I didn't know you did that," that means you are not telling all current clients about the services you offer. If they don't know, they won't bring you that piece of their business—and they won't make referrals to friends and colleagues. I want to show you some systematic ways to avoid the heartbreak of "*Idintnoyadiddat* Syndrome*.*"

> "*Our research has shown that interaction is what clients want--and that it's also the best route to profitability for advisors in terms of winning more assets and referrals.*"[2]
>
> *–Hannah Shaw Grove and Russ Alan Prince*

5. Make the Service Call Part of the Daily Routine

What I am about to tell you is simple, easy-to-understand, but hard to do, day after day, week after week, year after year. When you read the half-dozen dumb ideas for keeping clients you will think to yourself, "Duh! I knew that! In fact, I practice these ideas all the time." If you really do—congratulations! I'll bet you have a thriving successful business.

More business has been lost because the customer felt neglected, ignored, or unappreciated than for all other reasons combined. But how can you stay in contact with clients from your book of business so they don't feel taken for granted, neglected, ignored, and unappreciated?

It's simple: you should systematically contact your clients *regardless of market conditions*. If the market declines dramatically and bad news is on the horizon, make a special effort to get in touch with your most valued clients—*even if you just spoke with them last week.*

Your voice is the difference between you and some discount brokerage firm. Your clients do business with you because they know you, they like you, and they trust you to help them do the right thing. The number one complaint about brokers is not performance; it's that clients don't hear from them enough. You also need to make your clients feel special by keeping it personal, as well as professional. Remember and acknowledge their birthdays, their anniversaries, their children's' names and ages, their parents' and siblings' names, as well as their primary hobbies and interests. This kind of attention and interest can pay off—not only in potential friendship but also in additional business.

My suggestion is to make periodic service calls; that is, simply call your clients. Try to listen more than you speak. Say something along the lines of, "Hi Bob. Tom Rowley with ABC Corp—your Chief Retirement Office."

[Check in on their personal concerns. Ask the relevant questions—and then listen.] "How's your golf game? How's your daughter's soccer league team doing? How'd your wife's charity lunch for the Garden Club go?"

[Close with a couple of reminders about what you can do for them.]

"I'm just calling to let you know I'm here for you if you need me or have a question about lowering taxes or retirement planning. If I don't know the answer, at least I know where to find the answer to any personal financial question or problem you may have. I'll let you go, but stay well and stay in touch! Bye."

Financial advisors have told me they do the birthday call, the anniversary call, or even an ABC method. Some of your clients' last names start with the letter A, some with B, some with C, and so on through the alphabet. There are 26 letters in the alphabet. There are also 52 weeks a year. That means you can call everyone twice. Now you probably don't have too many clients whose last name starts with a Q, X, Y, or Z, but probably quite a few start with M (A trivial pursuit note: M is the most popular letter to start a last name in America).

The point is, calling clients from your book of business is critical to maintaining contact with your clients. Develop a plan or a system so it becomes a regular part of your process and less of a chore.

"I was talking to a futurist the other day..." Here is a phone call opener that you might try with your clients. I developed this opener after going through a Consultative Sales Approach (CSA) program (Note: you allow them time to set the agenda). "I was listening to a futurist the other day and he challenged us to bounce ideas off clients. I value your opinion and want your take on it. This futurist was saying layoffs are part of a larger trend that will take workers (especially older workers) off the payroll. Eventually few people will 'work' for a company;

however, many will become consultants to the process. Now, I'm not saying he is right, but what if he's on to something? What would you do? Tell me about the trends in your industry."

6. Appreciate Your Clients

Likewise, regularly set up client conference calls and client appreciation/retention luncheons, which convey the sense that you care about your clients—not just about the money they give you to invest. Conference calls should include a guest speaker and should never be longer than 10 to 15 minutes. These calls should be held at a convenient and comfortable time of the day. Remember to call clients to remind them of the date and time at least three days prior to the call, and be sure to follow up with them within two to three days after the call takes place.

Client appreciation luncheons may include a guest speaker or could be built around a theme or topic of interest to clients. You must be in attendance—but now is not the time to push products or make sales! Asking key clients to bring a friend (who is not already your client) is a great way to meet potential prospects! Follow up within four to five days after the lunch with a brief note to both clients and prospects. "Thanks for coming. I'd love to speak with you soon."

7. Use "Oh, by the way...": The Art of Getting Referrals

One of the topics that came up again and again as I talked to people in this business was referrals, referrals, referrals. Getting people to provide you with the name of someone else who may need your assistance is the key to referral success. There is nothing magical about getting referrals—it has to be an everyday, every person, and every phone call event.

You might try what I call the "Oh, by the way" method. Tape some of these phrases by the phone and see which ones work for you. You can also call it *subliminal advertising*.

> "Oh by the way... "
> "Sorry I had to put you on hold...I was helping someone
>   with an IRA rollover."
> "Do you know anyone
>   ...who has recently switched jobs?"
>   ...who moved into town recently?"
> "What did you do with the money from your old job?"

Build Your Business with New Prospects

In Chapter 10, *Defining and Finding the Ideal Client*, we discussed that the goal of prospecting is to build up the audience of people, your target clients—the people in the niche you've decided to focus on, the people for whom you want to be CRO. Before prospecting, here are three important questions to ask yourself:

1. What is your response to the question, "Why should I do business with you?"
2. Does the prospect understand and value the benefits of my services?
3. What information do you need to know to determine that the person you're speaking to is NOT a prospect?

Winning at the Prospecting Numbers Game

Prospecting for clients is based on questioning; however, questions are not all that is required for a good prospecting strategy. Remember, prospecting is a numbers game. Even professional baseball players are only successful at getting on base 30 percent of the time. These athletes are the best in their field and yet they actually fail consistently seven out of ten times! Why don't they get the fear of failure? Because they understand it's a numbers game. In the sales profession, a 20 to 30 percent success rate is good. When you can secure two to three appointments from every ten prospects or leads, you are doing a good job. Just keep getting up to bat.

Four Steps to Prospecting Success

1. *Prepare*. Prospecting is a contact sport. You must be prepared. Top salespeople have regular phrases and statements they use to generate interest. They are also prepared with a list of common objections and responses to handle any resistance the prospect or gatekeeper throws at them. This preparation comes from practicing and from making numerous calls to prospects.

2. *Track*. Use an index card system, three-ring binders, a manila file folder system, or a computer system. Any system works as long as you use it.

3. *Make the time to prospect*. Top salespeople allocate a certain percentage of their week to prospecting. Regardless of their workload, they put a priority on prospecting and follow through.

4. *Set goals*. One advisor told me the main reason he has been more successful prospecting than most of the other reps is because he sets goals for himself every week. He has goals for the number of contacts he makes and the number of appointments he sets. Basically, he said he works as many hours as it takes to hit his goals.

8. Position Yourself in a One-Minute-or-Less Elevator Speech

I've seen this personal introduction called the "elevator speech" or the "personal mission statement." Call it whatever you like; it works to present your unique story. Writing down a position statement and marketing yourself via this brief professional profile will help you define and distinguish yourself as you answer the question, "What do you do?" Your professional introduction should include four sections that answer these questions:

- *Who are you?* Describe what you do. Use "er" and "or" words (a CRO is a problem solver, advisor, educator, etc.).

- *What do you believe?* State how you feel about helping others achieve their financial goals. People relate to advisors who share their values. Here you might define your feelings about retirement, about helping people achieve their goals, or about making their money last a lifetime.

- *Why are you credible?* List your credentials (lead with those that distinguish you). People expect you to have the right designations. They want someone who recognizes and actively participates in a larger definition of service and contribution (community service, military service, charitable work, boards, associations, etc.).

- *What do you do for your clients?* End strong by explaining the benefits of prospects working with you.

Prepare a succinct and benefit-oriented, problem-solving "story" about what you do in preparation for the next step: heading out to network with a population of people that includes a large percentage of your ideal clients.

9. Use Questions that Keep Prospects Intrigued

Since your prospects may not know they've got a problem, this is where I could cite the fact that most Americans aren't saving for retirement. Of course, their problem is they don't have you! How do you help them discover that they need your help?

You do it by asking questions. The best way to differentiate yourself at the outset of a conversation with people you do not know is to tap into their curiosity. The less someone knows you, the less time you have to talk.

Certain questions provoke curiosity. Pose the classic question, "Guess what?" Pose that simple question to ten people; you can safely assume that nine will respond, "What?" You need to harness your prospects' curiosity.

Work your elevator speech backwards into provoking a question. For example,

"I work with people to help minimize the biggest risk they face with their life savings." Chances are good that this prompts, "What is that?" as a reply. *Curiosity piqued and permission to continue granted.*

Try to give prospects a glimpse of a few provocative pieces of information—just enough so that they'll want to continue the conversation to find out more. "When reviewing IRAs, I usually see two types of problems that require immediate attention. Aren't you curious what those two things are? Once you have the prospects' attention, you can begin to guide them toward the next stage of the process.

Questions you ask during your presentations should never sound like interrogations by Sergeant Joe Friday of *Dragnet* fame. They should be preceded by phrases such as:

> *"Explain for me if you will..."*
> *"Let me ask you this if I might..."*
> *"Could you help me with...?"*
> *"Could you expand on that for me?"*
> *"I'm interested in learning about..."*

These types of phrases soften the approach and allow the person to elaborate on an answer. The next thing to remember is the discipline of quiet. Resist the urge to jump in and present. Instead, question more. Use statements such as:

> *"Tell me more."*
> *"Please go on."*
> *"Elaborate on that for me, please."*
> *"I'd like to know more about that."*
> *"Please continue."*

And when they touch on a need, have them embellish and quantify that particular essential—and then have them discuss the implications. Use the all-time best question when needed. "Why?" It is short, simple, and nearly foolproof.

Your job is to ask questions, *listen*, ask questions, *gather information,* ask questions, *understand motives,* ask questions, *understand values,* ask questions, and *understand goals and dreams* (For a list of additional prospecting questions, see Figure 14.1).

10. Use the Naperville Approach

Another strategy to help build your book of business is what I call the "Naperville Approach." Naperville is the fastest growing city in Illinois. One of

FIGURE 14.1	Prospecting Questions

Gather Information
"What prompted you to look into this?"
"How do you see this happening?"
"How does that process work now?"
"What challenges does that process create?"
"What challenges has that created in the past?"

Uncover Motives
"How did you get involved in…?"
"What kind of challenges are you facing?"
"With whom have you had success in the past?"
"With whom have you had difficulties in the past?"
"What are your expectations/requirements for this product/service?"
"What process did you go through to determine your needs?"
"What would you like to see improved?"
"How do you measure that?"

Clarify Values
"What's the most important priority to you with this? Why?"
"What other issues are important to you?"
"What are the best things about that process?"
"Can you help me understand that a little better?"
"What does that mean?"

Understand Goals
"What goals would you like to see accomplished?"
"Why is that important to you?"
"What other items should we discuss?"
"What do you see as the next action steps?"
"What are your thoughts?"
"Who else is involved in this decision?"
"What could make this no longer a priority?"
"What's changed since we last talked?"
"What concerns do you have?"

the reasons for the growth is the number of job transferees who move there. These transferees arrive with no banking or brokerage relationships and may need a great deal of help to get acclimated to their new surroundings. Many transferees are probably starting new jobs as well. That means they may be looking for retirement savings solutions that address what to do with the money from their old plans.

Are you wondering where to meet these people? *American Demographics* magazine consolidates such research and survey information in their column "Datadog." Approximately one-half of the country's moves take place between Memorial Day and Labor Day, 42.2 percent are corporate relocations. According to an Atlas survey, "Fifty-seven percent of owners and 37 percent of renters bought furniture within 12 weeks of moving. Thirty-five percent of homeowners and 40 percent of renters bought bedding, 72 percent of those within three weeks after their move. Fifty-five percent of homeowners purchased at least one appliance when they moved. Twelve percent of all moving homeowners bought a car; 66 percent of these car buyers made the purchase within four weeks after moving into their new abode."[3]

Start by prospecting relocation companies, movers, or realtors. They may be able to refer you to people who are new to the area. Also watch your local business news sections that list newly hired business leaders, many of whom may have come from someplace else.

Relocation in retirement is on the horizon for many Baby Boomers. Nearly six out of ten are likely to move to a new home for retirement, whereas the 1999 Del Webb Baby Boomer survey of those aged 48 to 52 indicated that only 31 percent had plans to move during retirement.[4] Compared to past Boomer research, this demonstrates a rising interest in relocation among Boomers looking to retire.

11. Engage in CRO Networking

The most successful networkers are people who have learned to listen with interest to other people. In networking, we are selling ourselves. It's less about trying to be *interesting* and more about being *interested* in the person we are talking to. As CROs, we must convince people that we understand them, and that we are trustworthy and are worthy of their support. The best way to do this is to listen. Establish contact by showing genuine interest in people. Their attention to you is dependent upon your willingness to listen to them. Do not start off a relationship by talking about yourself. Find out what is important to the other person. Everyone has something special to offer—the type of work they do, an unique accomplishment. Be attentive and sincere. Nothing will kill a relationship faster than false sincerity.

Like matchmakers, master networkers thrive at bringing individuals together. They mentally connect new contacts with others. They listen for hints or subtle cues in conversation to establish mutually beneficial relationships. While matchmakers are focused on love, networkers are focused on creating value.

Mentally connect new contacts with others. Determine how each person could benefit from other contacts. The connection process is highly proactive and takes time and energy, but the payoff can be invaluable.

If someone mentions a problem, think about solutions—and think in terms of people. The most effective and unobtrusive way to make a connection is to include both in an email introducing them and mentioning what they can do for each other. Remain active only until the relationship can survive without your help. Once you have made the connection, disappear. The value of a network grows in proportion to the number of users. So, dig deep to create a successful networking program. Building such a network increases your value in an ever-expanding community of people who know you and respect your abilities.

Networking is the skill of stringing enough contacts together to reach your objective. Networking produces information and relationships. Relationships plus information equals power. If you are seeking clients, referrals are your best sources, and networking those contacts is a powerful way to build those referrals.

There are three types of networks that merit your attention:

- *Personal:* This cross-section of people you know will have interests and experiences in all kinds of subjects. These individuals are decentralize but connected through overlapping membership. More people build their business through the personal networks than any other way. I've heard a number of advisors say they met the client because, "His kid and mine played soccer together," or, "His brother married my cousin." They find someone who knows someone who can get them to someone they want to meet.

- *Associations:* Associations are people bonded together through shared values and ideas. For example, a writer's association would include all types of writers (copy, technical, fiction, and nonfiction). Although there are distinct differences and problems associated with the different types of writing, such an association provides many opportunities for networking since all writers have things in common. Any country club, service club, retiree center, or religious organization is really an association of people.

- *Targeted Professional:* These networks are more focused. They target the same level within a specific field, which gives you more of a rifle approach with groups like the Pilot's Union, the Society of Nuclear Engineers, the Association of Women Accountants, etc. Join an organization allied to those areas you think might interest you. Check *Gale's Encyclopedia of Associations*. You'll be amazed at the choices.

Here are some proven steps for networking:

1. *Develop a plan.* Whatever your needs, they are best satisfied by developing a strategic plan to get you there. What are you trying to accomplish? What organizations or associations would best satisfy the plan's execution? Research those people you wish to contact within the organization. Maintain records of the results of each contact, and follow through.

2. *Seek out events with relevant organizations.* Set a target for attending—once a month, once per quarter, etc. Join a networking/lead referral club. Attend one or two events a year that are out of your normal parameters. Consider parallel industries and attend their events as a source for strategic professional alliances.

3. *Research the organizations and identify the best people.* Some organizations will get you to your goal faster. Within any organization, identify the most likely prospects within that group. Find out who does what, who works in what specialty, etc.

4. *Prepare (in writing) and practice verbally delivering your quick personal introduction (appropriate to the event).* It doesn't have to be anything fancy. Use the person's name, if possible. For example, "Hi, Bill... I'm Tom Rowley with ABC corp., in the Retirement Plan Marketing Area."

5. *Follow these steps to initiate a conversation.* Prepare the elements you want to be able to say, even under pressure. See Figure 14.2 for helpful conversation starters and enders.

Your Networking Checklist: Before, During, and After

Before the Event...

1. Set clear objectives and goals.
   - Specify people you want to meet or number of discussions you want to have.

FIGURE 14.2	**Networking Phrases Toolkit**

Opening Questions are designed to initiate a conversation with someone.
- "How long have you been involved with this organization?"
- "Have you been to a meeting here before?"
- "What do you think of the event so far?"
- "How do you know the organizer of the event?"
  (Note: Ask only one question at a time. You're trying to initiate conversation, not grill the suspect.)

Value Statements are designed to focus on your products/services in terms of the value it delivers to your clients.
- "I educate my clients about the current winds of change in the workplace and how they can use some simple financial building blocks to weather the storm."
- "I help my clients meet their lifetime goals using the appropriate financial strategies."
- "I work with people to help minimize the biggest risks they face with their life savings."

Follow-Up Statements are designed to generate permission to be in touch for future discussions.
- "Can I give you a call next week to set up a time to talk in more detail?"
- "Would you like to get together on Friday and work through the idea?"

Exit Statements are designed to mark closure and give both parties a chance to move on to other conversations.
- "Nice meeting you. Will I see you at the next meeting?"
- "Well, that sounds exciting. Best of luck with that."
- "I'll let you get back to... I enjoyed meeting you."
- "It's quite an event. We should probably keep moving. I enjoyed talking with you, Sue."

• Designate number of post-event meetings you want to schedule.

2. Prepare your attitude to be completely positive (no "tradeshow cynicism").
   • Focus on being *interested*, and less on being *interesting*.

At the Event...

1. Work toward your objectives and goals.
   • Proactively initiate discussions.
   • Use your prepared and practiced introductions and initiating statements.

2. Send the right message.
   • Face the person completely.
   • Smile.
   • Be energetic.

3. Ask open-ended questions.
   • Listen completely (without the intent to respond immediately or display your knowledge).
   • Allow small gaps of silence (in many cases, the other person will fill the pauses with more information—sometimes extra information that's useful).

4. Give your undivided attention to the person in front of you.
   • Avoid wandering and scanning eyes (your goal is one-on-one attention).
   • Answer cell phones and pagers after you're no longer engaged in the conversation.

5. Deliver your value statements (when appropriate).

6. Maintain your networking attitude until the end of the event.

7. Complete positive follow-through (It's show time—literally).

After the Event...

1. Evaluate your networking performance.
   • Review against your objectives and goals for the event.

2. Follow-up with appropriate individuals.

- Use written form as soon as possible (handwritten note, email, or letter).
- Phone, if appropriate.

3. Begin to seek out your next event.
   - Set a target (once a month, quarter, etc.).
   - Join a networking/lead referral club.
   - Attend one or two events a year that are out of your normal parameters.
   - Consider parallel industries, and attend their events.

Use Every Tool to Grow Your Business

Growing your retirement business requires mindful and consistent practice of the basics: asking good questions, listening, and caring about peoples' answers, asking for referrals as an ongoing part of your business, and meeting new people in the areas populated with your ideal clients. Provide education, connect with people moving to the area, and polish up your positioning statement. Whether with clients or prospects, use these proven tactics, informational tools, and approaches to build your business. Then, sharpen skills and knowledge by continuing your education as CRO.

Chapter 15

CONTINUING YOUR EDUCATION AS CRO

"A good book is the life blood of a master spirit."
- *John Milton*

Believe it or not, we've just scratched the surface. The Chief Retirement Officer must be an ongoing student of the emerging trends in our business as well as what's on the minds of clients. Like the weather map, the financial terrain regarding your clients' retirement is constantly in flux.

New and revised legislation, shifting markets, product refinements, new offerings, and even jobs forecasts are all part of the financial weather map you need to consider. Understanding what's happening in these areas will improve your capabilities as the key leader of your clients' financial retirement team.

You'll want to stay abreast of the somewhat specialized retirement programs discussed briefly in this chapter. In addition, you'll want to stay in touch with your clients and their changing needs and concerns. This chapter will briefly address the big picture resources for staying on top of the relevant news trends that will color your clients' thinking. We will also cover the basics of some of the less common retirement funding programs. Not every CRO will deal with clients who are facing such specialized needs. Still, it's good to know about these programs in case you do encounter clients with these pressing needs. I've limited this discussion to the basics since it will be important for you to access the specific technical details on a timely and ongoing basis through continuing education programs and written resources from your firm.

Staying on top of all these changes is critical for the long-term success of your clients' retirements, and by extension, for your success as CRO.

Addressing the Big Picture

At the end of my talks, many financial advisors ask me, "What do you read to stay current?" Or, "Where do you read about the trends?" Once someone asked me, "I think I've developed the right plan to protect my clients from the storm—but where do I find information about the *storm*?"

In one sense, there's nothing new under the sun. The basics of accessing good information is a given, although the media may change. Scanning Web sites or reading business publications—*The Wall Street Journal, Barron's, Business Week, Forbes, Fast Company*—will keep you abreast of the big changes, not only in the financial industry but also in the bigger social and economic picture. Throughout the book, I've referenced specific articles that I uncovered in my readings, commentary that expands on the story we're telling.

In the last section of this book, I've included chapter notes, an appendix, resources for continuing education, and a bibliography. There, I've tried to include all the books, magazines, research reports, and studies that I've used to support the ideas comprised in this book. Many of the references are from general business news sources, or even "consumer" news outlets like *Newsweek* or *Time*. Other sources are more specifically geared to the financial industry. To do your job as CRO, you need to be conversant with both outlets.

Read What They Read

Good client relations stem from understanding your clients' needs and being genuinely concerned in them. Many of your clients are reading the same consumer and business publications you are. By paying attention to current news stories, you can create valuable springboards for conversations or even a reason to make a service phone call to check in on a trend that you think is particularly timely.

Beyond these shared news sources, you need to look at who your customers are and what they read. If you specialize in clients from a particular region, then you probably both read the local newspapers. If there's a local business paper, read that, too. If you specialize in an industry, say, airline personnel, then read the trade magazines, newsletters, or e-letters of that industry to stay current of the trends and concerns of your chosen client niche.

Some advisors even specialize in serving employees from a specific company. Carving out this specific niche means regularly accessing the public information, press releases, media mentions, and internal PR that is reasonably available, as well as maintaining stellar relationships with internal sources of information.

Whatever your specialty, get on the mailing lists (and email lists) of the publications, reports, Web sites, and forums that are targeted to your key niche of clients. Go to their conventions and trade shows. Visit the Web sites that cater to them. And yes, this is in addition to all the technical reading you do about the specific trends in the financial industry.

Watch for Trends

There's a certain art to reading the media for trends, but in very general terms, if you start to see an issue crop up in three or more varied sources, it's probably worth your attention. Addressing troubling trends proactively and head-on with your clients will certainly go a long way toward enhancing your credibility with them while positioning you as a CRO worthy of a long string of referrals. Imagine your clients saying, "My CRO called to check in after he'd seen several articles about the layoffs in the widget manufacturing industry. He's really paying attention. You should let him help you with all your IRA rollover headaches."

Specialized Retirement Vehicles

In the rest of this chapter, I want to highlight a few of the less common retirement investment-related programs that are likely to increase in importance and visibility if current trends continue to develop. Being aware of the basics of some of these specialized plans can benefit you in several ways.

First, you might mention relevant terms, in passing, to select clients. Let's say you're meeting with a client, who happens to be a teacher, and she's approaching retirement. You mention DROP plans—just in passing. "Did you realize that school districts are asking some of their senior teachers to stick around after they're fully vested in their pension plans? Teachers then can participate in what's called a DROP plan to increase their retirement dollars. This allows fully vested teachers to 'retire' from the pension plan but remain working for a predetermined period of a few years, while accumulating additional retirement funds in a DROP account that will earn interest." Your client may dismiss this notion. But two years later, when she is asked to stay on and participate in a DROP plan, you already have planted the seed, enhancing your credibility and confirming your expertise. You may be able to build on that relationship with your teacher-client to take DROP rollovers into IRAs, not only for your client, but for her colleagues as well.

Second, as a larger percentage of the population approaches retirement, people will learn quickly just what retirement surprises are lurking in their workplace-sponsored accounts. Do most of your clients really know what makes up their retirement accounts? I'd venture to say as many do as those who read their summary plan descriptions. These can be complicated programs, and your expertise in helping people unravel their complexities is exactly the value-added service that sets the CRO apart.

We will move through this last section from the most common to the lesser-known retirement funding vehicles.

Roth IRAs

While they're still less common than the tax-deferred IRAs, no discussion of IRAs would be complete without the Roth IRA. I've gone into some detail on Roths because they are the most common of the "specialized" retirement programs we discuss in this chapter.

As I mentioned in Chapter 9, *How to Get Clients to Take Action*, the Roth IRA was created as a result of the Taxpayer Relief Act of 1997. The main advantage of the Roth IRA is that the earnings grow tax-deferred while qualified distributions are tax-free (because money is put into a Roth on an after-tax basis). Additionally, minimum distribution rules do not apply and contribution limits are the same as IRAs.

Conversions
To convert a traditional IRA to a Roth IRA, the client's modified adjusted gross income must be less than $100,000. The limit is the same for married couples as for single individuals. Generally, if filing status is "married, filing separately," your client cannot convert a traditional IRA to a Roth IRA. There is an exception: if one spouse lives apart for the entire year, the couple can file separate returns and still be eligible for a conversion.

Only IRAs can be converted to Roth IRAs. Therefore, distributions from an employer's retirement plan require a two-step process:

1. Roll to an IRA.

2. Convert to a Roth IRA.

Partial conversions of an IRA are permitted; unfortunately, you can't separate taxable from nontaxable IRA dollars for conversion purposes. Here are a couple of rules of thumb for when *not* to convert:

- Don't convert if, in order to pay taxes on the conversion, the client needs to tap the IRA, which triggers the ten percent early distribution penalty on the amount taken out to pay taxes.

- Don't convert if the conversion amount pushes the client into a higher tax bracket for the year of the conversion. Remember that a partial conversion of the IRA may avoid this.

Distributions

Distributions from Roth IRAs are taxable (with possible penalties) unless "qualified." A qualified distribution passes two tests: the *five-year* and *type-of-distribution* tests. Passing both is necessary for a tax- and penalty-free distribution.

- *The five-year test*: The money must be held in a Roth IRA until January 1 of the fifth year after the Roth IRA was established (January 1 is not the anniversary date).

- *Type-of-distribution test*: There are four reasons for a qualified distribution: reaching age 59 1/2, death, disability, or "qualified first-time homebuyer."

Some distributions may be taxed but avoid penalties. Taxable but penalty-free distributions include: paying unreimbursed medical expenses greater than 7.5 percent of adjusted gross income; paying medical insurance premiums after losing a job; paying qualified higher education expenses for yourself, your spouse, your children, or your grandchildren; and distributions that are part of a series of substantially equal payments.

Distribution Order

The Roth IRA may contain dollars from different sources: regular contributions, conversion contributions, or earnings. The amounts may get different tax treatment upon distribution, and so it is important to know which dollars come out first. Distributions from a Roth IRA are assumed to come from the categories listed below in the following order (Remember, when applying distribution rules, treat all Roth IRAs as one):

- Annual contributions are withdrawn at any time, with no tax or penalty.

- Conversions (taxable portion) apply when the total of withdrawals from all Roth IRAs exceeds the total of annual contributions to Roth IRAs. Clients must still wait five years, or be over 59 1/2, or take the money for a qualified reason (death, disability, first-time homeowner) to avoid the ten percent penalty.

- Conversions (nontaxable portion) may be withdrawn at any time, with no tax or penalty.

- Each subsequent conversion may be withdrawn, in order, with the taxable portion coming out.

- Earnings must still wait the five years, or be over 59 1/2, or take the money for a qualified reason (death, disability, first-time homeowner) to avoid the ten percent penalty.

Death of a Roth IRA Owner

Only beneficiaries of Roth IRAs are required to take distributions. Just like the traditional IRAs, the rules depend on who inherits the Roth IRA. Spouse beneficiaries can elect to treat the Roth IRA as their own IRA. A non-spouse beneficiary has two options:

- *Five-Year Rule.* Distribute the entire account by December 31 of the fifth year following the year of the owner's death.

- *Life Expectancy Rule.* Distribute over the life expectancy of the beneficiary. The beneficiary must decide by December 31 of the year following the year of the death, or the five-year rule kicks in. The five-year rule also conveniently allows the beneficiary to satisfy the five-year hold rule for tax- and penalty-free withdrawals.

The life expectancy rule may require distributions before the Roth IRA has existed five years. However, distributions come out in the order listed above, and so earnings come out after all the contributions. The life expectancy distributions should be a small percentage of the overall value of the Roth IRA so that any distributions of earnings will probably be beyond five years. The ten percent early distribution penalty does not apply to post-death distributions.

Public Sector Employee Trends

As I noted earlier, the changes in demographics are having acute effects on the workplace, causing a shortage in qualified workers and the need for managers to prepare for the retirement of employees through better planning. The demographic "brain drain" pressures will affect all sectors of the economy. One of the first sectors to see the effect will be public sector employers. Let's look at what is happening in that industry as a prelude to what may happen elsewhere.

403(b) Market

A 403(b) plan, first established in 1958, is a retirement savings plan that is funded by employee contributions. 403(b) plans are not "qualified plans" under the tax code, but are generally tax-sheltered arrangements that can be used by tax-exempt 501(c)3 organizations. Think schools, hospitals. They can only invest in annuities or mutual funds.

Tax-exempt organizations and other nonprofit groups can now offer both the 403(b) and 401(k), but public schools must continue to offer only 403(b) plans. Organizations often offer another retirement plan as well, a 457 plan (a deferred compensation plan). One nice benefit of the 457 plan is that there are catch-up contributions missed in earlier years.

Something else you may encounter is a 403(b) plan to which employer contributions are made, referred to as Title 1 403(b) plan or a master 403(b). To establish a Title 1 403(b) plan, the organization executes a 403(b) master plan document. Therefore, you should look for the summary plan description (SPD) given to the employees.

Sounds complicated? Imagine what it is like for your clients! The 403(b) market will go through many changes over the next couple of years. Remember, where there is change, you will also find opportunity—making this an especially important market to keep tabs on.

Deferred Retirement Options Programs (DROP)

Deferred Retirement Option Programs, or DROP plans, first established in the mid-1980s, are becoming increasingly popular retirement options for public safety plans. Expect that, eventually, most public safety plans will include some type of DROP feature, and the use of DROP may spread to private sector employers.

Traditional public employee pension plans were designed to provide long-tenured, high-paid employees an incentive to retire earlier through their vesting function (a calculation based on years of service and age). When these employees become fully vested in their pension plan, the amount of their annual benefit from the plan is so close to their current annual income that they have little financial incentive to continue to work. This is particularly true for public safety employees (who may lack the physical stamina to keep up with their demanding jobs at later ages) as well as teachers.

During the teacher surpluses of earlier years, many school systems tried to get more experienced (thus, higher paid) teachers off the payroll to make way for less experienced (and less expensive) replacements. However, in many instances employers found that they have thereby discouraged some of their most loyal and productive employees from continuing to work. Also, schools are struggling for ways to retain and identify hard-to-find teachers in subjects such as math and science. An employer adopts a DROP plan to address both issues.

In general, DROP plans allow participants that are fully vested in a pension plan (satisfying service and age requirements) to "retire" from the pension plan (stop accumulating benefits), but remain working for a pre-determined period of time (generally less than five years).

The plan makes payments to employees' DROP accounts. The accounts earn interest. Once employees complete the DROP service period, they are fully retired and can access their pension and DROP accounts. DROP money can be rolled to an IRA. These lump sums can be quite large. For example, in the city of Milwaukee's plan, some senior staffers accumulated more than $1 million lump-sum payments.

During the post retirement period, a DROP provides the employee with more control (investment, beneficiary, and distribution) than a defined benefit (DB) plan. It also adds a level of complication to the process of retirement planning, a good reason to have a CRO.

Trend: DROPs are designed to address the problem of institutions suffering "brain drain."

Executive Level Compensation

As payroll continues to move from a fixed cost to a variable cost, pay packages will become more and more creative. (Read: complex. It means your clients will need the help of their CRO more than ever.) Companies may provide benefits for a select group of management or highly compensated employees with non-qualified, deferred compensation plans.

Non-Qualified Deferred Compensation Plan

Variable pay means that even employees will need to think like free agents. They will be paid on the results they achieve. The result of moving payroll costs from a fixed cost to a variable cost for corporations means that, for many of your clients, more of their compensation will be variable, even if they are full-time employees. Bonuses, commissions, and pay-for-performance will become a greater part of the pay packages. Therefore, make sure you do not overlook the planning power of the non-qualified deferred compensation plan.

Non-qualified deferred compensation plans are a fancy name for a simple concept. It's deferred because you defer compensation for a later time (retirement), and it's non-qualified because it isn't a retirement plan officially recognized by the Internal Revenue Service. The rules can get complicated from plan to plan. As a CRO, your value goes up because you will be able to help clients sort through all the rules.

The biggest issue is "constructive receipt." This means your clients defer income before receiving it, which means they can't get their hands on the money until retirement. The plan has to be selective—not all employees can be eligible. The key is to watch for employees with volatility in income (for example, salespeople) to be eligible.

In general, the employer is holding your client's money and promises to pay the income in the future. Be aware that it's an unsecured debt. Your client, the employee, is a general creditor of the employer. This is significant if the company gets into financial trouble. There are ways around this for the employee, but they are complicated. Whether your client works for a private company or a nonprofit organization, your client is likely to be able to postpone income taxes on earned income for years to come.

These may also be known as supplemental executive retirement plans (SERP), excess benefit plans or "Top Hat Plans." A nonqualified plan defers the receipt of taxable wages or bonuses until some future year when the employee may be in a lower tax bracket.

Nonqualified plans are either in the form of an individual contract or an employer plan. When a contract is involved, the contractual arrangements will vary to suit the parties' needs. There are many types of nonqualified compensation plans. Nonqualified deferred compensation plans may center on the use of life insurance. The most common types of insurance arrangements used in such situations are key employee insurance, group term, split dollar, and reverse split dollar. Here is a short list of what you may see:

1. *Excess Benefit Plans*. These "Top Hat Plans" may be either funded or unfunded by the employer. Funded plans are subject to ERISA's reporting and disclosure provisions. If the plan is funded, an employer's contributions are included in an employee's income in the year that the contributions are made.

   Unfunded plans mean that the employee assumes the risk that the employer may not be able to pay due to a merger, acquisition, insolvency, or other reason. An employee pays tax on the contributions when the benefits are distributed. An employer may assure that funds are available by using financing vehicles such as a Rabbi Trust, a corporate owned life insurance (COLI), or a Secular Trust.

Trend: while tax deferral opportunities are preferred, recent corporate scandals have made employees leery of programs that put their retirement funds at risk.

Excess benefit plan example: XYZ Corporation's qualified defined contribution retirement plan provides annual contributions equal to 20 percent of an employee's compensation for the year, subject to the qualified plan annual contribution limit. For senior vice president John, who has an annual salary of $300,000, the potential contribution would come to $60,000 (0.2 x $300,000). In 2002, however, only $40,000 can be added to John's qualified retirement plan account because that is the limit for the year. Fortunately for John, his employer credits the remainder of the contribution ($20,000) to an excess benefit plan.

2. *Rabbi Trusts*. Since many Top Hat plans are unfunded, Rabbi Trusts are often set up to provide additional security for the executive. Under the Rabbi Trust assets held are dedicated to provide participant benefits.

3. *Vested Trusts*. With this unfunded trust, the executive is not paid or taxed on any benefits until vesting occurs. Vesting usually is scheduled to occur in conjunction with a specific event, such as termination, takeover, or reaching a certain age.

4. *Secular Trusts*. A major distinction between Secular and Rabbi Trusts is that an employer's creditors cannot reach the money held in a Secular Trust during bankruptcy. As a result, an employer's contributions and earnings to a secular trust are generally taxable income to the employee.

5. *Deferred Bonus*. The simplest form of deferral is postponing the receipt of one year's bonus and having it paid over several annual installments, frequently over five years. An unfunded plan may defer receipt to defer the tax consequences of the bonus payment.

6. *Stock Options*. These were the darlings of the dotcom era. They are an agreement on the part of an employer to sell a certain number of shares of its stock at a given price to an employee within a specified period of time. Stock options may be qualified or nonqualified.

Trend: Variable pay for performance.

7. *Stock Appreciation Rights (SARs)*. SARs are a way to give an executive a stake in a company's growth (as reflected in its stock price) without actually having to invest in the company's stock. A SAR provides an executive with a cash bonus measured by appreciation in the value of company stock from the time that the rights are granted over a set period of time.

Trend: Variable pay for performance.

8. *Parachutes*. These can provide executives and/or employees with some benefits in the case of change of ownership or corporate control.

- *Golden parachutes* provide executives with a financial soft landing in the event that a takeover results in their discharge. Employers agree to pay amounts in excess of executives' usual compensation in the event of a change in ownership.

- *Silver parachutes* provide benefits to employees in the event of ownership change.

- *Tin parachutes* provide severance payments for rank-and-file employees that kick in if a hostile takeover costs employees their jobs. It is used as a defensive maneuver because having a greater numbers of payments can add up to a larger total package, even if individual payments are less.

- *Pension parachutes* increase retirement payments to employees in the Pension Plan. These become activated only after a change of corporate control results in the automatic termination of the company's retirement plan.

Trend: The desire to protect an organization or its leaders from suffering in takeovers.

9. *Discount Option Plans*. These plans are growing in popularity with not-for-profit employers because of their flexibility in meeting needs such as tax preferred performance bonus, supplemental executive retirement benefits, and volunteer tax deferred compensation. They are tools for executive recruiting and retention.

Trend: The competition faced by not-for-profit organizations, and their increasing professionalization.

Maintaining Your Edge by Continuing Education

Obviously there is much to learn—and vigilance is required to stay current. Lifelong education is a key factor that separates true CROs from their peers who choose not to go to the trouble. From the big picture to the technical details, the best CROs take an inclusive approach to the information needed to do their jobs at the highest levels. These thumbnail sketches of specialized retirement funding plans connect to the trends we've been discussing since we first looked at *The Winds of Change*. Because we have the programs available, and because the workplace is being reshaped in dramatic ways, I think these specialty plans will gain importance as the social and economic shifts continue to unfold. You may want to start familiarizing yourself with these plans now and keep your finger on the pulse of all these monumental changes by using the resources listed in the following sections.

NOTES

Section 1

1. Joseph A. Schumpeter, *Capitalism, Socialism and Democracy* (New York: Harper Torchbooks, 1984).

2. Robert Reich, *The Future of Success* (New York: Alfred A. Knopf, 2001). *Many of my initial thoughts on change were corroborated when I read this recent book by Reich. For those who need a "prequel" to my book, Reich explains in detail the systemic changes we are experiencing.*

Chapter 1

1. *Economist*, "Nest eggs without the yolk," May 10, 2003, 59.

2. Ronald J. Ryan and Frank J. Fabozzi, "The Pension Crisis Revealed," *Journal of Investing*, Fall 2003, 43.

3. Robert Kuttner, "The Great American Pension-Fund Robbery," *Business Week*, September 8, 2003, 24.

4. "Nest eggs without the yolk," 60.

5. Stephen Taub, "Coming: Pension Crisis?" CFO Publishing Corporation, October 18, 2002, http://www.cfo.com/article/1,5309,7923,00.html (accessed January 3, 2003).

6. Anne Tergesen, "Negative Nest Eggs," *Business Week*, November 17, 2003, 158.

7. Kuttner, 24.

8. "Nest eggs without the yolk," 59.

9. "Nest eggs without the yolk," 60.

10. David M. Katz, "PBGC Chief to CFOs: Mind Your Liability," CFO Publishing Corporation, November 18, 2004, http://careers.cfo.com/article.cfm/3398564/c_3400615?f=home_todayinfinance (accessed November 30, 2004).

11. Robert Guy Matthews, "Retiree Costs Drive Big Change in Steel; Retirees Are Losers," *Wall Street Journal*, sec. A, April 25, 2002.

12. David Welch, "Pick Me As Your Strike Target! No Me!" *Business Week,* April 21, 2003, 68.

13. Robert Borosage, "At the Kitchen Table," The Institute for America's Future, http://www.TomPaine.com/scontent/9318.html (accessed November 17, 2003).

14. Robert Guy Matthews, "As Steel Industry Consolidates, Workers' Benefits Begin to Shift," *Wall Street Journal*, January 3, 2003.

15. For an updated list, see Crain's Business lists, http://www.chicagobusiness.com.

16. Janice Revell, "General Motors: GM's Slow Leak," *Fortune*, October 15, 2002, http://www.fortune.com/fortune/investing/articles/0,15114,373503,00.html (accessed January 3, 2003).

17. Danny Hakim, "Carmakers In for a Long Haul In Paying Retiree Health Care," *New York Times*, September 15, 2004.

18. Roger Lowenstein, "Detroit's Dilemma," *Smart Money*, September 2001, 55-56.

19. Lowenstein, 55-56.

20. Gary Radtke, on December 9, 1998, to the National Committee on Vital and Health Statistics, Subcommittee on Standards and Security, http://ncvhs.hhs.gov/981209t8.htm (accessed January 2, 2003).

Chapter 2

1. *Wall Street Journal*, "Number of Jobless Hits 20-year High," July 11, 2003.

2. Jon E. Hilsenrath, "Slump in Job Market Is Longest in Decades," *Wall Street Journal*, sec. A, January 13, 2003.

3. Carleen Hawn, "The Global Razor's Edge," *Fast Company*, February 2004, 27-28.

4. Hilsenrath.

5. Hawn, 27-28.

6. Alison Doyle, "Where Have All the Jobs Gone?" About, Inc., http://jobsearch.about.com/cs/careerresources/a/offshore.htm (accessed September 16, 2003).

7. Hawn, 27-28.

8. Hawn, 27-28.

9. Doyle, http://jobsearch.about.com/cs/careerresources/a/offshore.htm (accessed September 16, 2003).

10. Hawn, 27-28.

11. *Wall Street Journal*, "Outsourcing abroad draws debate at home," July 14, 2003.

12. *Wall Street Journal*, "Census sees a surge in Americans without insurance," September 3, 2003.

13. United Food and Commercial Union Workers, "Wal-Mart Quick Facts," United Food and Commercial Union Workers Union, http://www.ufcw.org/issues_and_actions/walmart_workers_campaign_info/facts_and_figures/walmartgeneralinfo.cfm (accessed November 15, 2004).

14. American Staffing Association, "Staffing Leads Job Growth," http://www.staffingtoday.net/staffstats/index.html (accessed November 15, 2004).

15. Wendy Zellner, "Coffee, Tea, or Bile?" *Business Week*, June 2, 2003, 56-58.

16. *Business Week*, "Cutting to the Bone," June 2, 2003, 56.

17. Employee Benefit Research Institute, "Employee Tenure," Employee Benefit Research Institute Education and Research Fund, 24, no. 3, (2003), http://www.ebri.org/notesx/0303note.htm (accessed April 7, 2003).

Chapter 3

1. Mitch Anthony, *The New Retirementality* (Chicago: Dearborn, 2001).

2. Financial Research Corporation, "Money on the Move: Strategies for Capturing Retirement Rollovers," Financial Research Corporation, June 12, 2002, pp. 11, 29.

3. Mitch Anthony, "The End of Retirement," *Research Magazine*, September 2004.

4. Sandy Aird, "Meet the Innovators," *Plan Sponsor*, December 2000.

5. Noam Neusner Wellner, "Pink-slip blues: Jobless pay takes work," *U.S. News & World Report,* November 5, 2001, 74.

6. Employee Benefit Research Institute, "EBRI Study on `Bridge Jobs': Older Americans Working More," Employee Benefit Research Institute Education and Research Fund, February 17, 1999, http://www.ebri.org/prrel/pr458.htm (accessed December 9, 2004).

7. "Traditional Perception of Retirement is Obsolete According to Comprehensive New Study," AIG SunAmerica, April 30, 2002, http://www.re-visioningretirement.com/PDF/press_release.pdf (accessed December 9, 2004).

8. Institutional Investor, Oct 2001.

9. American Association of Retired Persons (AARP), "The Aging American Workforce: Get Ready," AARP, http://www.aarp.org/money/employerresourcecenter/researchanddata/Articles/a2004-07-22-agingworkforce.html (accessed November 30, 2004).

10. Financial Research Corporation, 11.

11. Financial Research Corporation, 26.

12. Financial Research Corporation, 26.

13. Financial Research Corporation, 26.

Chapter 4

1. Spectrem Group, "Targeting High Balance Rollovers," 2001.

2. "IRA Growth Trends," *The Cerulli Edge*, June 2002, 12.

3. Spectrem, 2.

4. Financial Research Corporation, 14.

Section 2

1. H B Gelatt, *Creative Decision Making: Using Positive Uncertainty*, rev. ed. (Menlo Park, CA: Crisp Publications, 2003).

Chapter 5

1. Federal Emergency Management Agency and American Red Cross, "Family Disaster Plan," The American National Red Cross, http://www.redcross.org/services/disaster/0,1082,0_601_,00.html (accessed November 17, 2004).

2. This stress list was ranked by American Institute of Stress. Similar lists have been developed over many years, from Holmes & Rahe, 1967; Lazarus & Folkman, 1984; Kreiger et al., 1993. An alternative stress list is available at http://www.stresstips.com/lifeevents.htm (accessed November 18, 2004).

3. Alvin Toffler, *Future Shock* (New York: Random House, 1974).

4. Valerie Adler, "Little control = lots of stress: job stress in low-echelon jobs," *Psychology Today*, April 1, 1989.

5. Carol Kleiman, "Job search could take a new course," *Chicago Tribune*, January 13, 2002.

6. Some of the most helpful and groundbreaking work in the area of grief, loss, and stress includes the following:

Elizabeth Kubler-Ross, *On Death and Dying* (New York: Macmillan, 1969). *Kubler-Ross identified "five stages of loss" in her work with the dying. These five stages can be applied to anyone dealing with loss.*

John Bowlby, *Sadness and Depression* (New York: Basic Books, 1980).

Bowlby, of the Tavistock Institute of Human Relations in London, developed a three-phase outline of the process of separation.

J. Shep Jeffreys, *Coping with Workplace Change: Dealing with Loss and Grief* (Menlo Park, CA: Crisp Publications, 1995). *Jeffreys developed the "Unfinished Business Model" regarding storing unaddressed grief feelings.*

J.W. Worden, *Grief Counseling and Grief Therapy* (New York: Springer, 1991). *Harvard Psychologist Worden developed "four tasks of mourning."*

Stephen Fineman, *White Collar Unemployment and Stress* (New York: John Wiley and Sons, 1983).

Georgia Witkin, *Stress Relief* (New York: W. W. Norton, 2002).

Deborah Paddock, "After the Layoff: Job Search Strategies," *Career Information*

Center, 6th ed., Employment Trends and Master Index, vol. 13, (New York: Macmillan Library Reference, 1996), 80-85.

Fred Wish, "Adjusting to Job Loss," *Career Information Center, 6th ed., Employment Trends and Master Index*, vol. 13, (New York: Macmillan Library Reference, 1996), 102-108.

Chapter 6

1. http://www.zaadz.com/quotes/search (accessed December 9, 2004).

2. Zig Ziglar, *Steps to the Top* (New York: Pelican, 1985).

3. Paul Karasik, "The Four Fears," *On Wall Street*, August 2003, 65.

4. Olivia Mellan, "Hear, Hear!" *Investment Advisor*, May 2002, 119-122.

5. H.B. Gelatt's *Positive Uncertainty Approach* is elaborated in a number of sources, including:

H. B. Gelatt, "Positive uncertainty: A new decision making framework for counseling," *Journal of Counseling Psychology*, 36, (1989): 252-256.

H. B. Gelatt, *Creative decision making using positive uncertainty* (Los Altos, CA: Crisp Publishing, 1991).

H. B. Gelatt, "A new vision for counseling," *Counseling and Human Development*, 25 (1) (1992).

6. Matthew Benjamin, "Playing defense: Before a layoff, take stock of finances and prepare—just in case," *U.S. News & World Report*, November 5, 2001, 78.

7. Shaifala Puri, "As Layoffs Rise, So Do Age-Discrimination Charges," *New York Times*, March 18, 2003. http://query.nytimes.com/gst/abstract.html?res=F30616F93C550C7B8DDDAA0894 DB404482&incamp=archive:search (accessed December 8, 2004).

Chapter 7

1. Harry Beckwith, *The Invisible Touch* (New York: Warner Books, 2000).

2. Bill Bachrach, "You Can Handle the Truth," *Investment Consulting News*, January 2001, 2.

3. AIC, "What is a Financial Advisor?" AIC Client Services, http://www.aic.com/en/main/home.asp?Disp=http%3A//www.aic.com/en/financial_to olkit/toolkit_professional_advice.asp (accessed April, 2004).

4. <u>Black's Law Dictionary,</u> 7th ed., ed. Bryan A. Garner, (St. Paul, MN: West Group, 1999), 640.

5. U.S. Department of Labor, "Fiduciary Responsibilities and Liability," U.S. Department of Labor, http://www.dol.gov/dol/topic/retirement/fiduciaryresp.htm (accessed July 13, 2004).

6. John Lohr and Ian Lohr, "On Fiduciary Responsibility, the Definition of Fiduciary, and Prudence," *Investment Management Consultants Association*, January-February 2004, 19-24.

7. Donald Moine, "Are You a Fiduciary?," Morningstar, August 15 2003, http://advisor.morningstar.com/advisor/doc/article/0,8832,3149,00.html (accessed July 20, 2004).

8. Kristi Cook, "The Growing Mutual Fund Scandal and its Effect on the 403(b) Marketplace," *NTSAA Legislative Advisor*, January/February 2004, 19-20.

9. International Financial Risk Institute, "Prudent Man Rule," International Financial Risk Institute, http://riskinstitute.ch/00012513.htm (accessed November 18, 2004).

10. U.S. Department of Labor, "What is the Significance of Being a Fiduciary?," U.S. Department of Labor, May 2004, http://www.dol.gov/ebsa/publications/fiduciaryresponsibility.html (accessed July 20, 2004).

11. Bachrach, 2.

Chapter 8

1. Todd Duncan, interviewed by editor, "High Trust Brokerage," *On Wall Street*, February 2004, 88.

2. John Naisbett, *High Tech, High Touch: Technology and Our Search for Meaning* (New York: Broadway Books, 1999).

3. Scott West and Mitch Anthony, *StorySelling for Financial Advisors* (Chicago: Dearborn, 2001), 111-112.

4. David Irwin, "The Future of Wealth Management," *On Wall Street*, March 2004, 96.

5. Duncan, 88.

Section 3

Chapter 9

1. Lao-tzu, quoted by Brian Johnson, http://www.thinkarete.com/quotes/by_teacher/lao-tzu/1/ (accessed November 19, 2004).

2. Ron Lieber, "What the Hell is Audix?," *Fast Company*, February 2002, 52.

3. "Retirement Markets Dominate," *The Cerulli Edge*, May 2002, 3.

4. Financial Research Corporation "Destroy Silos for IRA Rollover Success," Financial Research Corporation, http://www.frcnet.com/frc/research/articles/art_mkts_ira_silos.asp (accessed July 12, 2002; site now discontinued).

5. Financial Research Corporation, 25.

6. Financial Research Corporation, *IRA Rollover Trends* (Boston: Financial Research Corporation, November 2003).

7. AARP, "Baby Boomers Envision Their Retirement: An AARP Segmentation Analysis," http://research.aarp.org/econ/boomer_seg_1.html (accessed December 9, 2004).

8. AARP.

Chapter 10

1. West and Anthony, *StorySelling for Financial Advisors*.

2. National Commission on Entrepreneurship, "Five Myths About Entrepreneurs: Understanding How Businesses Start and Grow," RenderX, March 2001, 5, http://www.renderx.com/~renderx/myths/en/art_original.pdf (accessed November 22, 2004).

3. Similar comparative statistics are reported in "Redefining Main Street for 2000." http://www.nationalbusiness.org/NBAWEB/Newsletter/487.html (accessed November 19, 2004).

4. AARP.

5. Van Kampen Investments, "IRA Rollover Opportunity: Client's Distribution, "Van Kampen Investments, 2002.

Chapter 11

1. Abraham Maslow, *Toward a Psychology of Being*, 3rd ed., ed. Richard Lowry, (New York: John Wiley, 1998).

2. Joseph Pine and James Gilmore, *The Experience Economy* (Boston: Harvard Business School Press, 1999).

Chapter 12

1. International Revenue Service, "Survivors, Executors and Administrators," U.S. Department of the Treasury, 2003, http://www.irs.gov/pub/irs-pdf/p559.pdf (accessed December 9, 2004).

2. International Revenue Service, "Individual Retirement Arrangements," U.S. Department of the Treasury, 2004, http://www.irs.gov/pub/irs-pdf/p590.pdf (accessed December 9, 2004).

3. International Revenue Service, "Introduction to Estate and Gift Taxes," U.S. Department of the Treasury, September 2004, http://www.irs.gov/pub/irs-pdf/p950.pdf (accessed December 9, 2004).

Chapter 13

1. "Retirement Markets Dominate," *The Cerulli Edge*, May 2002, p. 1.

2. Michael K. Stein, "The Kaleidoscopic Retirement," *Journal of Financial Planning*, March 2001, 36-37.

3. Social Security Administration, "Benefit Percentages for Early Access," Social Security Administration, http://www.socialsecurity.gov/retire2/retirechart.htm (accessed November 23, 2004).

4. Social Security Administration "Standard Retirement Ages," Social Security Administration, http://www.socialsecurity.gov/retire2/retirechart.htm (accessed November 23, 2004).

5. Anthony, *The New Retirementality*.

6. EBRI-ERF Retirement Security Projection Model Study, "Can America Afford Tomorrow's Retirees?," *EBRI Issue Brief*, November 2003.

7. Aon, "Long-Term Care," Aon, http://www.aon.com/us/busi/hc_consulting/employee_benefits_cons/executive_bene-fits/benefit_plans/long_term_care.jsp (accessed November 10, 2004).

8. Aon, "Long-Term Care."

9. Centers for Medicare and Medicaid Services, "Your Medicare Coverage" U.S. Department of Health, http://www.medicare.gov/Coverage/Home.asp (accessed November 23, 2004).

10. Scudder Kemper Investments, "1999 Guide to the Generations," *American Demographics*, May 2000, 54.

11. Dave Blackmon, "Don't Throw Around Retirement Income," *Senior Market Advisor*, March 2003, 69-76.

12. Donald Jay Korn, "Not Your Mother's Retirement Products," *Financial Planning*, October 2003, 75-79.

13. Korn, 75-76.

Chapter 14

1. West and Anthony, *StorySelling*.

2. Hannah Shaw Grove and Russ Alan Prince, "Streamlining an Advisory Practice, Part 2," *Financial Advisor*, June 2002, 37-39.

3. Robert Libbon, "Dear Data Dog: - - U.S. Census Bureau's report on geographical mobility of Americans" *American Demographics*, January 1, 2001.

4. "Baby Boomers Worried About Money for Retirement," *SeniorJournal*, June 18, 2003, http://www.seniorjournal.com/NEWS/Features/3-06-18delweb.htm (accessed December 4, 2004).

APPENDIX

A Snapshot of Baby Boomers as Prospects
(With research sources)

If you took a snapshot of your prospects, what would they look like?

About a third are well off. They are earning large salaries with one or both spouses working. They have invested assets and may be lucky enough to receive an inheritance from the preceding generation. Another third will have to save harder. They are saving, not investing. They may have to extend their work life at least five years beyond their current expectations in order to meet their retirement goals. They may be house rich but cash poor. The last third, largely female, will have few investments and little savings but will receive their retirement assets from the proceeds of a life insurance policy, if they are fortunate.

What do the prospects look like, and what are they worried about?

There are endless surveys, opinion polls, and research reports on the Baby Boomers. I have pored through them and compiled a snapshot of the Baby Boomer prospect. Following this summary, you'll find capsule summaries and references from the actual sources I used.

These Baby Boomers are among the top one percent of wealthiest Americans. They are corporate employees who work on average a 52-hour week. Most own only one home and do not have full-time domestic help. They own two automobiles. Their children are enrolled in public schools. They rarely buy fine art or jewelry and would describe their childhood background as "poor, lower middle class, or middle class."

They plan to work in retirement, perhaps in a new career or part-time, mostly because they feel work provides a stimulus. They look forward to retirement to spend time with their spouse or significant other and travel.

They feel they have enough knowledge to make appropriate financial decisions on their own. Although many are not working with a financial advisor or broker, one-third believe they would benefit from professional advice. Some believe that financial institutions are not interested in having them as clients.

Most are happy and satisfied with life. They have outgrown the instability and turmoil of their youth and now experience great satisfaction with marriage, as well as pride in their children and their work. Contrary to popular polls, they are not worried about aging and plan to grow old gracefully.

A survey conducted in 1999 by the AARP, "Baby Boomers Envision Their Retirement," showed that Baby Boomers possessed traits falling into one of five distinct groups: Strugglers, Anxious, Enthusiasts, Self-Reliants, and Today's Traditionalists. You can tell by the labels that the last three groups are your prospect bases, comprising 68 percent of the total.

Their main concerns are: "not having enough money to do what I want, not being healthy enough to do what I want, and having to go back to work because I will need the money."

Baby Boomer Research Sources and Annotations

Harris Interactive and Allstate, "Second Annual Allstate Retirement Reality Check Survey Reveals Baby Boomers' Financial Worries Increasing" (2002), created by Allstate in conjunction with Harris Interactive.

Using a random digit dialing methodology, Harris Interactive polled 1,400 people born between 1946 and 1961 with household incomes ranging from $35,000 to $100,000. 52 percent reported worrying about having sufficient retirement funds—up from 29 percent in 2001.

- Worries about health care costs rose from 39 percent to 67 percent in the same time period.
- And when it comes to fears about retirement, female Boomers are more concerned about not having enough money (55 percent vs. 48 percent of males), about Social Security disappearing (54 percent vs. 40 percent of males), and about getting sick (52 percent vs. 45 percent of males).
- 74 percent say they are financially prepared for retirement.

- *Reality Check:* 59 percent expect to carry some form of debt into retirement, whether it is a mortgage (27 percent), car payments (36 percent), or credit card balances (28 percent).
- 66 percent feel they have enough knowledge to make appropriate financial decisions on their own.
- *Reality Check:* 62 percent report that choosing the right kind of investment is a challenge.
- 34 percent believe that financial institutions are not interested in having them as clients.
- While 56 percent are not working with a financial advisor or broker, 33 percent believe they would benefit from doing so.

Roper Starch Worldwide, Inc. and AARP Research, "Baby Boomers Envision Their Retirement: An AARP Segmentation Analysis," February 1999. http://research.aarp.org/econ/boomer_seg_1.html (accessed December 27, 2002).

The Strugglers (9 percent). With the lowest incomes of the five groups, the Strugglers are mostly female (64 percent). Strugglers are saving virtually no money for retirement because they have no money to save. The majority say they look ahead to their later years with very little sense of optimism.

The Anxious (23 percent). The Anxious individuals are best characterized by their sense of apprehension when they look ahead to later years. Although they fall below the average Baby Boomer household income level, they do try to put some money aside for retirement but do not expect to be rewarded with financial well-being when they retire. Many do not expect to be able to stop working. Also, they express concerns about health care coverage during their retirement years.

The Enthusiasts (13 percent). The Enthusiasts couldn't be more eager to reach their retirement years and do not plan to work at all during retirement. They envision having plenty of money as well as plenty of time for recreation. For them, retirement promises to be a time free of the rigors of working.

The Self-Reliants (30 percent). This group boasts the highest income and educational level of any of the five groups. The Self-Reliants have the resources to save money and are aggressively putting money into retirement-oriented investments. They want to continue working at least part-time when they retire. What motivates them is not the pay but rather the interest and enjoyment that work provides.

Today's Traditionalists (25 percent). Having a stronger sense of confidence and less uncertainty regarding Social Security and Medicare than the other four groups, Today's Traditionalists plan both to work and to rely on these programs during retirement.

The *Baby Boomer Report* is an annual opinion survey commissioned by Del Webb, the active adult brand of Pulte Homes. Del Webb, "Annual Survey: Baby Boomers Worried About Money for Retirement," June 18, 2003. http://www.seniorjournal.com/NEWS/Features/3-06-18delweb.htm (accessed December 4, 2004).

America's Baby Boomers are concerned about having enough money for their retirement and envision work remaining a big part of their lives. Del Webb surveyed people between the ages of 44 and 56 who were either employed full-time or seeking full-time employment. This group represents the segment of the Baby Boomer generation that is actively planning for their retirement and whose retirement attitudes and perceptions provide a window into future retirement trends.

Will Baby Boomers Continue to Work in Retirement?

- 43 percent of those surveyed plan to continue working in retirement with another 44 percent unsure whether or not they'll work. "The survey also tells us that 76 percent of those surveyed are not confident they will have enough income in retirement," said Dave Schreiner, vice president of active adult development for Pulte Homes. "So this high level of uncertainty may be attributed to financial insecurity and an uneasiness over the need to work in retirement."

- 51 percent of those planning to work in retirement expect to start a second career, with 37 percent working part-time in their primary career. Interest in starting a second career seems to be increasing by leaps and bounds among Boomers. In the 1996 Del Webb Boomer study, only 13 percent of those who said they were planning to continue working in retirement planned on beginning a new career. Of those who will continue working in retirement, the average age that they'll stop working completely is 70, with 29 percent of them never planning to stop working at all.

Why Keep Working?

While financial concerns loom large on the minds of the surveyed Baby Boomers, when asked to rank the top four reasons why they'll continue to work, at the top of the list was mental stimulation.

1. Mental stimulation (52 percent)
2. Don't think savings and Social Security will provide enough income (46 percent)
3. Keeps me physically active (39 percent)
4. Enjoy working (33 percent)

"You can see that today's active adults want to remain connected to the world around them," said Schreiner. "Gone are the days when retirees were looking for a chance to slow down and disconnect from the world. Now, people want to remain active, both physically and mentally, and want the stimulus provided by being involved in the work place and the issues facing the world."

What are Their Top Concerns About Retirement?

Boomers are no different from many others, with money and health worries topping their list of concerns in retirement. When asked to rank their top three concerns, those surveyed said:

1. Not having enough money to do what I want (54 percent)
2. Not being healthy enough to do what I want (52 percent)
3. Having to go back to work because I'll need the money (25 percent)

Despite these concerns, Boomers do look forward to:

1. Having more time to spend with their spouse or significant other (45 percent)
2. Traveling (44 percent)
3. Having more free time (29 percent)

Survey, U.S. Trust

Of individuals born between 1946 and 1964 who are among the top one percent wealthiest Americans, this survey revealed that typical affluent Baby Boomers fit the following description:

• Average a 52-hour work week and take four weeks of vacation per year

- Most often travel domestically on vacation
- Own only one home, valued at less than $500,000
- Own two automobiles, with the average value of each less than $30,000
- Intend for their children to receive the majority of their pre-college schooling from public schools
- Do not have full-time domestic help
- Rarely or never buy fine art or jewelry
- 68 percent of wealthy Baby Boomers describe their childhood background as "poor, lower middle class, or middle class"

Nearly half (48 percent) of affluent Baby Boomers earned their wealth from corporate employment. This contrasts with the older affluent, half of whom earned their wealth through their own businesses. Less than one-third of affluent Baby Boomers (31 percent) earned their wealth from a private business, and only 11 percent of Baby Boomers surveyed cited inheritance as their primary source of wealth.

In 1995, 76 percent of those surveyed worried about inflation versus 57 percent today. The proportion of affluent Baby Boomers concerned about rising taxes decreased from 73 percent in 1995 to 51 percent today, and the number anxious about not being able to save enough money for retirement declined from 68 percent to 49 percent today. Similarly, in 1995, 56 percent worried about losing their job or going out of business versus 35 percent today.

Research on United Methodist Baby Boomers

The results of the survey indicate that most United Methodist Baby Boomers are happy and satisfied with life. They appear to have outgrown the instability and turmoil of their youth and now experience great satisfaction with marriage, as well as pride in their children and their work and hope in their faith.

The "me" ethic of this generation has been replaced by the "we" ethic, as Boomers adopt a new "family values" ethic. Since 95 percent of the men and 90 percent of the women surveyed intend to remain with their spouses for a lifetime, perhaps by this time the worst marriages have already dissolved.

Contrary to popular polls relating to aging Boomers, United Methodist Boomers are not worried about their aging and plan to grow old gracefully. Now that the majority of them have reached mid-life, middle age is "in," and the youth culture is "out."

It is interesting that the United Methodist Boomers carry negative baggage concerning views of their own generation. This is not unusual: it is a learned response. The media and other institutions (including the church) labeled this generation selfish, irresponsible, radical, and seeking instant gratification. People have a tendency to live out their lives fulfilling the expectations of others. As a result, only 44 percent of United Methodist Boomers view their generation in positive terms. Most people surveyed had little good to say about their generation, yet 95 percent of those surveyed indicate that they are quite satisfied with their lives.

While four out of five survey respondents expressed a positive outlook about the future, many United Methodist Boomers expressed a growing concern about the escalating cost of health care, violence in our society, and saving enough money for retirement.

Richard H. Gentzler, Jr. and Carolyn S. Poole, *The Pulse of United Methodist Baby Boomers* (Nashville: The United Methodist Church, 2000). http://www.gbod.org/ministries/adult/boomerbook/default.html

What Will the Boomer Prospects Want?

Developing a Decumulation Strategy for the Income Phase of Retirement

According to a report in *Fund Marketing* published March 4, 2004, Fidelity Investments plans on launching a centralized account designed to serve Baby Boomers preparing for retirement. With this account, Fidelity hopes to enhance its position in the battle to capture rollover assets as they shift from retirement plans into retail accounts. After consolidating cash and various other investments within this one account, investors will be in a position to utilize tools that will help them calculate tax-efficient methods of taking distributions without depleting retirement savings. Plan Sponsor's "News Dash" reports that no fee IRAs, satisfaction guarantees, free trades, and investment advice are all used as forms of differentiation to help persuade investors to choose one form over another.

American Century guarantees that investors will be satisfied with its Personalized Rollover Service. If the investor is dissatisfied, American Century will not only fix the situation but also send the individual a $50 American Express gift card or a one-year subscription to *SmartMoney Select.com*. The guarantee applies even if an investor does not complete the rollover with American Century. American Century rollover specialists also have the ability to offer personalized investment advice to rollover investors through services powered by Financial Engines.

"NewsDash," *Plan Sponsor*, March 12, 2004
http://www.plansponsor.com/nd_type1/?RECORD_ID=24608 (accessed
December 3, 2004).

According to a report in *Plan Sponsor*, a survey by Greenwich Associates
found that only 35 percent of DC plan participants use the Internet information
tools provided by their companies, and the percentage using the tools to their full
extent is likely a fraction of that. The importance of investment education and
advice are widely recognized by plan sponsors, but participants would rather
make their choices based on in-person contacts. This has been recognized by plan
sponsors: the number of companies offering investment advice via the Internet
dropped from 55 percent in 2002 to 43 percent in 2003. Despite the demand for
in-person advice, the costs of providing this service, via telephone or face-to-face,
can be economically challenging.

"Survey: Plan Internet Users Few and Far Between," plansponsor.com, 18
February 2004, http://www.plansponsor.com/pi_type10/?RECORD_ID=24290
(accessed December 3, 2004).

RESOURCES FOR CONTINUING EDUCATION

In addition to the books and specific articles listed above and in the endnotes, I recommend the following list of business, professional and trade magazines, journals, newspapers, and numerous Web sites. These sources comprise a sampling of important resources that should be part of every CRO's reading list. They offer updated statistics and new information, so peruse these sources regularly to watch for trends and breaking research.

Periodicals:

American Demographics
Barron's
Business Week
CFO.com
EBRI Issue Brief (print)
Economist
Fast Company
Fortune.com
Financial Advisor
Financial Planning
Investment Advisor
Investment Consulting News
International Financial Risk Institute
Investment Management Consultants Association
Journal of Financial Planning
Journal of Investing

NTSAA Legislative Advisor
On Wall Street
Research Magazine
Senior Market Advisor
Smart Money
U.S. News & World Report
Wall Street Journal

Internet Resources:

http://www.AARP.org
> The American Association of Retired Persons is the source for reams of research and other reports about Baby Boomers, their current issues, and their lifestyle changes.

http://advisor.morningstar.com/home.asp

http://www.aaltci.org
> American Association for Long Term Care Insurance.
> The Mission of the American Association for Long Term Care Insurance is "To heighten awareness among consumers for the need
> and benefits of owning private LTC insurance by enhancing the
> expertise and developing high standards of professionalism among agents, brokers and financial advisors."

http://www.staffingtoday.net/staffstats/index.html
> American Staffing Association's Web site will keep you up to date on issues relating to temporary workers.

asri.com's bi-weekly Layoff Report Google news. Click on "advanced news search," type "layoffs" in the "Find results with all of the words," and type the name of the state where you want to search in the "location" box. If you'd like to search within a specific city or other narrower geographic area, add its name as a search term along with "layoffs."

http://www.bls.gov/oco/
> The Bureau of Labor Statistics' Occupational Outlook Handbook is every other year and lists careers/occupations.

www.bls.gov/oco/cg/
   The Bureau of Labor Statistic's Career Guide to Industries is a
   companion resource that provides valuable background and employment
   projections.

http://www.comingofage.com/
   This is a marketing firm that specializes in communications to Baby Boomers.

http://www.ebri.org/
   Employee Benefit Research Insititute offers a wealth of information and original research reports for financial professionals.

http://www.efmoody.com/longterm/longtermoverview.html
   E. F. Moody's site lists resources on long-term care and aging issues. Moody
   teaches California's continuing education course for Long-Term Care.

http://www.freeerisa.com/
   FreeERISA provides free access to pension and benefit plan information.
   Searches can be done by state, zip code, or business name.

http://www.hrlive.com/
   HRLive provides a weekly summary of layoff announcements gathered from
   news services across North America.

http://www.plansponsor.com/
   PlanSponsor.com provides breaking financial and workplace news briefs
   along with in-depth analysis.

http://www.firstresearch.com/
   First Research publishes background information on more than 140 industries.
   Individual reports cost $99 each; an annual subscription for a single user is
   $675.

http://www.ici.org/statements/res/index.html
   Investment Company Institute publishes invaluable research on the investment
   industry. As stated on the home page, "The Institute publishes a reference
   book, two regular research newsletters, and a variety of research and policy
   reports that examine the industry, its shareholders, or industry issues."

http://www.spectrem.com/info.shtml
   Spectrem Group offers high-level strategic research on retirement and the
   financial industry as well as an array of information products.

BIBLIOGRAPHY

In addition to the works cited in the endnotes, the following resources formed a necessary part of my preparation as background for writing this book. As a CRO, if you are committed to the ongoing project of your own continuing education, you may find that some of these sources provide helpful insights to improve your professional capabilities.

American Association of Retired Persons. "Aging Baby Boomers: How Secure Is Their Economic Future?" Washington, D.C.: AARP, 1994.

Anthony, Mitch. *The New Retirementality*. Chicago: Dearborn, 2001.

Beckhard, R., and W. Pritchard. *Changing the Essence*. San Francisco: Jossey-Bass, 1992.

Beckwith, Harry. *The Invisible Touch*. New York: Warner Books, 2000.

Berchem, Steven P. "The Flexibility Factor: ASA's Annual Economic Analysis of the Staffing Industry." American Staffing Association, http://www.staffingtoday.net/staffstats/annualanalysis03.htm (accessed November 22, 2004).

Bernheim, B. Douglas. "The Adequacy of Personal Retirement Saving: Issues and Options." In *Facing the Age Wave*, 30-56. Stanford, CA.: Hoover Institution Press, 1997.

— —. How Much Should Americans be Saving for Retirement?" *American Economic Review*, 90, no. 2 (May 2000): 288-292.

Bowlby, John. *Sadness and Depression*. New York: Basic Books, 1980.

Butrica, Barbara A., Howard M. Iams, and Karen E. Smith. "It's all Relative: Understanding the Retirement Prospects of Baby Boomers." Working paper, Boston College Center for Retirement Research, Chestnut Hill, MA. Available online at http://www.bc.edu/centers/crr/papers/wp_2003-21.pdf.

Covey, S. *The 7 Habits of Highly Effective People*. New York: Simon and Schuster, 1989.

Downing, Neil. *New IRAs and How to Make Them Work for You*. Chicago: Dearborn, 2002.

Engen, Eric M., William G. Gale, and Cori E. Uccello. "The Adequacy of Retirement Saving." *Brookings Papers on Economic Activity*, no. 2. 1999.

——. "Effect of Stock Market Fluctuations on the Adequacy of Retirement Wealth Accumulation." Draft, available from the authors.

Ferguson, Karen, and Kate Blackwell. *Pensions in Crisis: Why the System Is Failing America and How You Can Protect Your Future*. New York: Arcade Publishing, 1995.

Ferguson, M. "Paradigm Shift from Separation to Seamlessness." *New Sense Bulletin* no. 17, (1991): 4.

Fineman, Stephen. *White Collar Unemployment and Stress*. New York: John Wiley and Sons, 1983.

Gale, William G. "The Aging of America: Will the Baby Boom Be Ready for Retirement?" *Brookings Review* 15, no. 3 (Summer 1997): 4-9.

Garvin, David A., and Michael A. Roberto. "What You Don't Know About Making Decisions." *Harvard Business Review* (September 2001): 108-116.

Gellat, H. B. *Creative Decision Making: Using Rational and Intuitive Techniques to Make the Best Decisions*. Los Altos, CA: Crisp Publications, Inc., 1991.

——. *Creative Decision Making: Using Positive Uncertainty* rev. ed. Menlo Park, CA: Crisp Publications, 2003.

——. "Positive uncertainty: A New Decision Making Framework for Counseling." *Journal of Counseling Psychology* 36 (1989): 252-256.

——. "A New Vision for Counseling." *Counseling and Human Development* 25, no. 1 (1992).

Gist, John R., Ke Bin Wu, and Charles Ford. "Do Baby Boomers Save and, If So, What For?" (Washington, D.C.: AARP, June 1999). Available online at http://research.aarp.org/econ/9906_do_boomers.pdf.

Grangaard, Paul A., and Larry Atkins. *The Grangaard Strategy: Invest Right During Retirement*. New York: Perigee, 2003.

Handy, C. *The Age of Unreason*. Boston: Harvard Business School Press, 1989.

Havemen, Robert, and others. "Have Newly Retired Workers in the U.S. Saved Enough to Maintain Well-Being Through Retirement Years?" Madison: University of Wisconsin.

Hebeler, Henry K. *J.K. Lasser's Your Winning Retirement Plan*. New York: John Wiley & Sons, 2001.

Hutchins, Larry. *Systemic Thinking: Solving Complex Problems*. Colorado: Professional Development Systems, 1996.

Jeffreys, J. Shep. *Coping with Workplace Change: Dealing with Loss and Grief*, Menlo Park, CA: Crisp Publications, 1995.

Kotlikoff, Laurence, and Alan J. Auerbach. "U.S. Fiscal and Savings Crises and Their Impact for Baby Boomers." In *Retirement in the 21st Century: Ready or Not?* edited by Dallas L. Salisbury and Nora Super Jones, 85-126. Washington, D.C.: Employee Benefit Research Institute, 1994.

Ronald Krannich and Caryl Rae Krannich. *Best Jobs for the 21st Century*. Manassas Park, VA: Impact Publications, 1998.

Kubler-Ross, Elizabeth. *On Death and Dying*. New York: Macmillan, 1969.

Land, G., and B. Jarman. *Breakpoint and Beyond*. New York: Harper Business, 1992.

Lohr, John, and Ian Lohr. *The Fiduciary Sale: The Director's Cut*. Orlando: Isle Press, 2003.

Maslow, Abraham. *Toward a Psychology of Being*, 3rd ed. New York: John Wiley, 1998.

Naisbett, John. *High Tech, High Touch: Technology and Our Search for Meaning*. New York: Broadway Books, 1999.

O'Shaughnessy, Lynn. *Retirement Bible*. New York: Hungry Minds, Inc., 2001.

Paddock, Deborah. "After the Layoff: Job Search Strategies." In *Career Information Center*, 6th ed., *Employment Trends and Master Index*, vol. 13. New York: Macmillan Library Reference, 1996.

Pine, Joseph, and James Gilmore. *The Experience Economy*. Boston: Harvard Business School Press, 1999.

Reich, Robert. *The Future of Success*. New York: Alfred A. Knopf, 2001.

Sabelhaus, John, and Joyce Manchester. "Baby Boomers and Their Parents: How Does Their Economic Well-Being Compare in Middle Age?" *Journal of Human Resources* 30, no. 4 (Fall 1995): 791-806.

Schaffner, Herbert A., and Carl E. Van Horn. *A Nation at Work 2003*. New Brunswick, NJ: Rutgers University Press, 2003.

Scholz, John Karl, Ananth Seshadri, and Surachai Khitatrakun, "Are Americans Saving 'Optimally' for Retirement?" Working paper, Department of Economics, University of Wisconsin, Madison, WI. Available online at www.ssc.wisc.edu/~scholz/Research/Optimality.pdf.

Schumpeter, Joseph A. *Capitalism, Socialism and Democracy*. New York: Harper Torchbooks, 1984.

Senge, P. *The Fifth Discipline*. New York: Doubleday, 1990.

Shrader, Ralph W. "Leadership in an Age of Uncertainty: The Trust Factor." Keynote address, FOSE 2002, Washington, D.C., March 21, 2002. Available online at http://www.fose.com/Keynotes/shrader.pdf.

Slott, Ed. *The Retirement Savings Time Bomb*. New York: Penguin Group, 2003.

Stevens, Paul. *Portfolio Careerism: Are You Ready?* Sydney, Australia: The Centre for Worklife Counselling, 2000.

VanDerhei, Jack, and Craig Copeland. "Can America Afford Tomorrow's Retirees: Results from the EBRI-ERF Retirement Security Projection Model." *EBRI Issue Brief*, no. 263 (November 2003). Available online at http://www.ebri.org/pdfs/1103ib.pdf.

West, Scott, and Mitch Anthony. *Storyselling for Financial Advisors*. Chicago: Dearborn, 2000.

Wheelan, Charles. *Naked Economics: Undressing the Dismal Science*. New York: W. W. Norton & Company, 2002.

Wish, Fred. "Adjusting to Job Loss." In *Career Information Center 6th ed. Employment Trends and Master Index*, vol. 13. New York: Macmillan Library Reference, 1996.

Witkin, Georgia. *Stress Relief*. New York: W. W. Norton, 2002.

Wolff, Edward N. "Retirement Insecurity: The Income Shortfalls Awaiting the Soon-to-Retire." Washington, D.C.: Economic Policy Institute, 2002. Available online at http://www.epinet.org/content.cfm/books_retirement_intro.

Worden, J.W. *Grief Counseling and Grief Therapy*. New York: Springer, 1991.

Yuh, Yonkyung, Catherine Phillips Montalto, and Sherman Hanna. "Are Americans Prepared for Retirement?" *Financial Counseling and Planning* 9, no. 1 (1998): 1-13.